# The Deeper Quest

# The Deeper Quest

D. Joseph Jacques

BOOKS

Winchester, UK
Washington, USA

First published by O-Books, 2012
O-Books is an imprint of John Hunt Publishing Ltd., Laurel House, Station Approach,
Alresford, Hants, SO24 9JH, UK
office1@o-books.net
www.o-books.com

For distributor details and how to order please visit the 'Ordering' section on our website.

Text copyright: D. Joseph Jacques 2011

ISBN: 978 1 78099 024 8

A CIP catalogue record for this book is available from the British Library.

Design: Stuart Davies

Printed and bound by CPI Group (UK) Ltd, Croydon, CR0 4YY
Printed and bound in the United States of America by Edwards Brothers Malloy

We operate a distinctive and ethical publishing philosophy in all
areas of our business, from our global network of authors to
production and worldwide distribution.

# CONTENTS

Dedication:

I dedicate this book to those who carry on.
Each one of you is vital to the cause.

# Preface

**With a squeal of rusty hinges** and rumble of iron chains, the ancient drawbridge falls open at your feet. The Grail Castle beckons you inside.

Like others before you, you hesitate, anxious to learn its many secrets, yet unsure of what will follow. The thought crosses your mind that this may be the moment for which you were born.

After a lifetime of challenges and disappointments, you will soon find answers that have long escaped you, answers pointing back to the origin of your people – perhaps to the mystery of existence itself. The questions that drove you here echo in your mind, unspoken yet insistent. Seeking their answers has already shaped your direction thus far. You know well that *whatever you seek with passion shapes your destiny.*

According to legend, one of the treasures that waits for you inside is a book. Some call it the *Book of Life*, a book of secrets from a forgotten past. Others warn that when you look at it, the pages are blank, the words write themselves as the worthy person performs great deeds. When someone else finds it, the words disappear so that a new story can take its place.

Either way, *the deeper quest* crosses the threshold to another world. Here you will find the cultural and spiritual depth of your ideals, knowledge that contributed in no small measure to making you who you are. Here you can lay claim to the spiritual roots that are your inheritance.

Other cultures might reserve such learning for masters and initiates, who veil their knowledge in secrecy.

Not here. The Western Way has no room for masters or initiates. Knowledge is for all who seek it. The search for truth defines who we are.

*Chivalry-Now*, the philosophical expression of these ideals, presents us with a reservoir of principles focusing on self-development, personal responsibility, and a treasure trove of thoughts dating back to a forgotten past. The process of acquiring that self-discipline and knowledge cannot be derived from a book, however, or many books. It comes through seeking it out directly, learning through experience, or not at all.

We call this process the *quest*.

By confronting the challenges of life as a journey of discovery through which we learn and grow, we experience the immediacy of life in the here and now, which is the core principle of *authenticity*. It is a journey that each of us is called to take alone. No book, not even this one, with its open drawbridge, can replace the trials of actual experience. Think of this book as a catalyst for thought.

The quest is different for every person who partakes in it. Individuality makes that certain. Nevertheless, it is wise to gain insight from those who came before, whose wisdom has survived the test of time. Transmitting such wisdom is the purpose of culture and tradition. When a culture fails to do that, it offers noise and very little substance, filling empty hearts not with joy but with longing, no matter what our material wealth or spiritual aspirations.

Each person's quest is a unique reflection of his or her life. Lessons to be learned are found at every crossroad, contributing to growth, purpose and integrity. These are the benefits of the quest, an adventure filled with meaning that, in the end, makes the world a better place. All we need do is see life for what it is, and live accordingly.

This book introduces cultural treasures that will illuminate and fortify your quest experience. Many are from times when people were closer to nature than we are now, a time when life was simpler and more reflective. Used properly, they provide insights for your journey, the legacy of those who passed this way before and bequethed what they learned for *our benefit*.

What you glean from their insights entirely depends on you.

No one can decipher life's meaning on your behalf. We start by acknowledging the obvious: *wisdom is found by the inquisitive mind*. We are called to learn from our every encounter with truth, and grow accordingly. That is what the quest is all about.

In the following pages you will confront the treasures and challenges of *Esoterica*, a collection of Western concepts that made us who we are, and lead us on the road to fulfillment.

The drawbridge waits for you to enter.

Welcome to the temple of *Esoterica*.

# Part I

## Esoterica–*The Quest for Knighthood*

# Introduction

**Truth has a way** of making itself known.

Whenever we confront it, its sublime nature sparks a recognition that resonates in our souls.

The experience can be profound, even life transforming. Why? Because for creatures who think, ponder and reflect, incorporating truth into our lives validates who we are.

The rational mind plays a significant role in what it means to be human. It values what is true in order to function properly. Beyond this practical role, relating to the grandiosity of truth also informs us that there is more to life than our everyday routines. We come face-to-face with the significance of human life, with its moral demands and ability to judge. We conclude that our lives should count for something more than the measurement of our consumption.

We instinctively know that our relationship with truth is *life-affirming*. The religious heart understands that, but so does the heart of the dedicated scientist, philosopher or mystic – or anyone who feels inspired by the beauty of music, a setting sun or the perfectly crafted phrase. When we allow it, this affirmation takes hold of us for a moment. It authenticates the reality we are part of.

The questions that follow are these: Is it possible to hold onto this affirmation for more than a moment? Can we incorporate it as part of our everyday lives? Can we use it to find meaning in everything we experience?

In other words, will a relationship with truth make us more *authentically human*?

Such questions are not new. We find them universally articulated in myth and literature reaching back to prehistoric times. In Western culture, they play a central role in stories that involve the *quest*.

The quest is a learning process through which heroes are born from incomplete persons. From the adventures of *Odysseus*, to the tales about *King Arthur's Knights*, to Tolkien's epic trilogy, *The Lord of the Rings*, the challenges of the quest describe a life-transforming process that adds vital components to who we are. Consider how just by changing our perspective to one that views life as an adventure instantly changes consciousness itself.

The concept is simple. When we embrace life as a quest, we engage in a spiritual journey through which we constantly learn and grow from everyday experience. We no longer distort what is best about our lives in order to fit dull routines, prejudice and stifling self-images. We no longer enslave ourselves to stagnant ideologies that take away the work and responsibility of forming our own decisions.

Instead, we willingly face the challenges of life boldly, deal with them heroically, and inject virtue in everything we do. We protect ourselves from whittling away our lives through meaningless routine, and reward ourselves with purpose that is worth living.

We need not search far to engage the quest that awaits us. All it takes is a moment's inspiration. As one Grail tradition tells us, the goal we seek is *down the road a little way, over to the left, and across the drawbridge.*

If the words and concepts in this book seem strangely familiar, as if they are part of you already, it is no coincidence. It is the nature of the quest to express in the language of our souls our deepest yearnings, symbols and moral imperatives. It connects the conscious mind to its own labyrinth of conscience to awaken what is there already. Whether this knowledge is innate, culturally embedded, or a mixture of both, matters little. What matters is that *it is part of us*. Raising it to consciousness, thereby bringing it to life, completes who we are. In this way, we are reborn.

The quest awakens the truth inside us to the truth around us.

It is a process integral to who we are. We call this truth *Aletheia*. (We will explore the richness of this term later.) Through the quest, we engage the world as a learning, and even sanctifying experience, filled with meaning and purpose. Knowing that we are uniquely and consciously part of the world around us places us exactly where we should be.

Remember – each age calls for its heroes because it needs their input and direction.

This is your invitation.

# Chapter I

# Opening One's Mind

*"...it is not permitted that we should trifle with our existence."*

So wrote **Edmund Burke**, the 18<sup>th</sup>-century, Irish/Anglo father of modern conservatism.

Although he was not referring to the quest as we define it, he amply expresses its serious intent. As living beings, the finite existence that we own should not be trifled with. Like the *parable of the talents* told by Jesus, in which we are condemned by the careless non-engagement of our lives, we are charged by what can only be described as a sacred mandate not to waste ourselves. What good are we if the miracle of our lives does not contribute to the world's betterment?

Life is existentially relevant for each of us, despite its confounding mixture of sadness, joy, mediocrity, challenge and final limitation. It is vitally important that we take that seriously – all the more because each of us represents a unique perspective. Living correctly is the only proper response for a being who is capable of thought, purposeful deed and moral reflection. Edmund Burke acknowledged this in another warning that we still hear quoted today:

*"The only thing necessary for the triumph of evil is for good men to do nothing."*

Around the same time that he wrote that, thousands of miles away, a radical insurgent named *Thomas Jefferson* spoke his mind as well:

*"...I have sworn upon the altar of god, eternal hostility against every form of tyranny of the mind..."*

Where did the severity of this hostile commitment come from? Jefferson tells us elsewhere, giving us a glimpse into what generated the energy of his life's work:

*"I sincerely believe in the general existence of a moral instinct."*

You might question why I cherry-picked quotes from political icons of opposing ideologies.

I did this to clearly illustrate, up front, the nature of the quest. No one owns truth in its entirety. No one can contain it. Bits and pieces show themselves where they will. It neither submits nor limits itself to the conjecture of anyone. Traditionalists like Burke and radicals like Jefferson, both virtuous men despite their conflict of opinion, demonstrate the eclectic nature of Western thought. Truth resonates piecemeal from many diverse perspectives. When we fail to recognize that, we shut ourselves off from the totality of truth and veer toward error and fanaticism. On the other hand, when we open our minds to diverse opinions, we uncover our greatest strength.

History shows us this as well. From gadfly philosophers like Socrates, to impoverished saints like Francis of Assisi; from church doctors like Thomas Aquinas, to humanists like Albert Einstein; from idealistic giants like Abraham Lincoln, to madmen like Frederick Nietzsche – we find sparks of value in them all. Incorporating truth into our lives wherever we find it is by definition the nature of the quest. That is and always has been the greatest strength of Western culture. Freedom of thought and the discovery it instigates is where authenticity begins.

Despite many claims to the contrary, truth does not come to us in a neatly wrapped package. In order to be real, it must be found fresh and new by each individual. That living relationship is what the quest is all about. It provides us thrilling clues and illuminating fragments that add significantly to our unique journeys, and glimpses of mystery that transcend formalized religion. Science may approach but never encapsulate it. In the political field, to suggest that truth is bi-partisan or non-partisan misses the point entirely. Impartial, objective thought can never be bound by the constrained and circular reasoning of parti-sanship.

We must never allow the truth we seek, the values we adhere to, and the virtues we extol to be distorted by dogmatic ideologies, distractions of convenience, or two-dimensional ideas of patriotism. Either we approach life directly, with existential awe and spiritual/humanistic reverence, *and learn from it,* or we get lost in the trappings of illusion.

\* \* \*

**One of the important lessons we learn** from our journey is that most of the problems we face are of our own making. As individuals and as a society we often ignore that simple fact in order to avoid responsibility. Unfortunately, by not admitting our personal involvement, we sustain and even propagate the problems that we suffer.

There are, of course, problems that are not directly of our making, such as disease or natural disasters. Our philanthropic response to such tragedies is often quite generous, heroic and immediate, rescuing the needy, healing the sick, rebuilding what was lost.

While more people die from car accidents, smoking, and chemical addiction than hurricanes, tornados, floods or even terrorist attacks, we respond more urgently to natural crises or foreign threats than to those that are of our own making.

Collectively, we have the intelligence and capacity to end

hunger, prevent many diseases, resolve conflicts before violence occurs, support equality and avoid the insanity of war. The reasons we do not are complicated. The most obvious comes from a lack of vision. In many and subtle ways we set ourselves against one another because of greed, selfishness, the lust for power, and political ideologies that thrive on contention. The problems continue to plague us despite our best intentions. They are too daunting, too prevalent, too complex and tightly embedded. Perhaps we even enjoy conflicts, and work to sustain them.

In light of all these problems, Chivalry-Now offers a simple, cost-effective, life-enhancing solution that would impact them all – one with which Burke and Jefferson might possibly agree.

Consider what would happen if people made more intelligent and compassionate choices in their lives, and exercised the self-discipline to perform them. Most of our social problems would vanish overnight, at little cost.

Imagine what would be possible if our best minds could then focus on solving the problems that are outside of our direct control, like disease and climate change.

Think how the world would be transformed if each of us exhibited something as simple as genuine courtesy in all our relationships.

Such positive steps transcend liberal and conservative thinking as we know them today. They provide commonalities that unite rather than divide – enjoining the very best of religion and humanism, tradition and science, thought and intuition. They replace the moment's transitory mix of pleasure and misery with a meaningful and positive obligation for the future.

* * *

As a philosophy or social ethic, Chivalry-Now can only exist in the hearts of those who live it. All else is just chatter or specu-lation. That includes the *12 Trusts* and *Esoterica* (which is the focus of this book). Chivalry-Now is a name for something deeply human that has evolved over millennia. It is a moral yearning that struggles to express itself – an impetus capable of fulfilling who we are, not only as individuals, but as a species as well. It calls for us to forge our own destinies.

The *12 Trusts* and *Esoterica* provide us with the cultural inheritance of a time-tested code built on the common sense wisdom of previous philosophical development. To be effective, however, we must consider them not as rules or commandments, but as catalysts for thought. The final teacher is the quest itself, which is the experience of life and the daily revelations from which we learn.

This book describes the teachings of *Esoterica*. It presupposes that the reader is familiar with the *12 Trusts* as expounded by the introductory volume, *Chivalry-Now, the Code of Male Ethics*. For those unfamiliar with this work, the *12 Trusts* are repeated here:

*Upon my honor,*

1   I will develop my life for the greater good.
2   I will place character above riches, and concern for others above personal wealth.
3   I will never boast, but cherish humility instead.
4   I will speak the truth at all times, and forever keep my word.
5   I will defend those who cannot defend themselves.
6   I will honor and respect women, and refute sexism in all its guises.
7   I will uphold justice by being fair to all.
8   I will be faithful in love and loyal in friendship.
9   I will abhor scandals and gossip – neither partake nor delight in them.
10  I will be generous to the poor and to those who need help.

11  I will forgive when asked, that my own mistakes will be forgiven.

12  I will live my life with courtesy and honor from this day forward.

By adhering to these 12 Trusts, I swear to partake in the *living quest* in everything I do.

For many people, this simple code of ethics is what Chivalry-Now is all about. The only ingredient they must add is their own personal resolve. If enough people do this, our culture would heal itself. The meaning of the Grail legends would be fulfilled and Western Civilization would slip back on course as the vanguard of reason and compassion.

It is only natural that some people will want more. The call of chivalry pulses in their veins, a thousand years in the making. They will want to know the deeper aspects of Chivalry-Now. Having glimpsed the heart of their own identity, they long to become knights in the truest sense of the word.

How, then, do we define *knighthood* in order to make it relevant for today? What would it require? Upon what would it be based?

The child in us might suppose that the title by itself is sufficient, without need to earn it. The accolade confers some kind of magical transformation that the world will automatically recognize and honor.

Like most of the illusions we confront everyday, such fantasy leads only to disappointment. Wishful thinking, even if it involves wearing a suit of armor, does not transform someone into a knight. Nor does a tap on the shoulder by some titled person, genuine or otherwise. In an age that hungers for real meaning, we must not allow today's concept of knighthood to be a thing of whimsy or vanity. It must be real and significant, or why bother?

Chivalry-Now offers this deeper quest to those who seek the validation of knighthood with all their hearts. Here we explore the conceptual roots of this possibility, some dating back to ancient Greece, others from more recent luminaries. If we imagine Chivalry-Now as an intellectual stream passing from antiquity to the present, we find a number of significant tributaries have added to its flow.

## Chapter 2

# The Foundation of Chivalry-Now

**Although Chivalry-Now returns** something that was lost, it is not a treasure lifted intact from an ancient grave, fixed and inviolate. It is, rather, the continuation of a time-honored development of thought, punctuated by historical highlights, that has frequently made Western culture progressively significant to the world. The earliest ideals that it represents, lingering in our collective conscience, comprise our noblest inheritance. It is time that we recognize them for what they are. It is time that we reclaim them, and nurture their blessings for all posterity. Indeed, the times require that we must.

Whereas Western culture is well known as the birthplace of the scientific method, democracy and capitalism – each of which has profoundly influenced the direction of the modern world – these are just the offspring of something more grand. They reflect the moral vision and generative impulse of the Western mind itself.

These qualities are overlooked as a tree is sometimes forgotten for its fruit. Their relevance and almost universal appeal are often slighted for the short-comings of their applications. Like people everywhere, we often fail to live up to our ideals – sometimes with terrible results. This does not detract from the ideals themselves. It indicates our failure to live up to them.

We are only human. Like all human beings, we experience a tension between our highest moral values and our baser inclinations. Some of us perform better than others. Some fail completely. While this might be seen and even condemned as hypocrisy, it actually portrays the confused, metaphorical battle between good and evil that wages in our souls.

This explains the contradiction in the United States Constitution that espoused freedom and allowed for slavery at the same time. This moral dichotomy reflects the birth-pains of high ideals caught in the process of actualizing themselves. The quest is a journey comprised of many steps, some of them backwards or slipping off the path, yet each of them in some respect vital. The haphazard nature of human progress is such that its gems and genius are always in the making – and marred by fallibility.

The birth pains continue. As history shows, freedom and slavery coexisted until respect for one brought bloody end to the other. Imperialism once flourished among Western nations, despite our respect for national independence, and still defines many of our political and corporate interests today. Closer at hand, we witness daily how love for neighbor is ignored when it competes with the bottom line.

Nevertheless, in the midst of our own shortcomings, we continue to struggle to create something grand. To complete this task, if it ever will be completed, we need to employ the midwife of understanding and new resolve.

Thanks to globalization, our task is no longer the experiment of a regional effort. It involves and affects all humanity. We must be open to the insights and judgments of other peoples as well. The purpose of life is not a competition, as many would have it. *It is a quest*. Each well-meaning path deserves to be respected and learned from.

We must always take care that our journey is not misdirected by hubris or ethnocentricity. None of us living today did anything to contribute to the *Age of Enlightenment* that defines so much of who we are. We are its beneficiaries. The achievements of Isaac Newton were his alone – not yours or mine. If culture were such that Newton's genius reflected the worth of us all, solely by accident of birth, then Hitler's depravity would be ours as well.

No. We are each judged by our own beliefs and actions, our contributions or lack thereof. If not, then freedom, which is the core of our Western make-up, is meaningless.

As our quest moves on, it does well to embrace *humility* as our closest companion. Without humility, our eyes are closed to the lessons before us.

Please remember, Chivalry-Now is a guide but not a vehicle. It can instigate thought, fortify and comfort, but will not do the work for us. Only *we* can do that. The smallest and greatest among us are charged with that same responsibility. As we embark on our quests we do well to chart the course of our own explorations, and learn from our mistakes as well as our successes. Our tools consist of reason, virtue, and that most demanding proposition of them all – *freedom*.

\* \* \*

**Reason, liberty, knowledge**, compassion, a desire for truth, a respect for equality and fair-play, generosity – these virtues comprise the impulse of Western philosophy from earliest times. They persisted and occasionally triumphed over the oppressiveness of ignorance, greed, superstition and bigotry. If not for those occasional regressions, which we contend with still, the West might consider itself exceptional indeed. Unfortunately, under the aegis of freedom no less, today's broken culture provides fertile ground for vice as well as virtue – despite the hope of many and the discipline of the few.

The germ of reason coupled with virtue first expressed itself for posterity in the intellectual soil of ancient Greece. Despite the endemic superstition of neighboring kingdoms, it blossomed with almost miraculous fervor, indelibly embedding itself in the Western psyche. In the short span of two hundred years, the genius of Socrates, Plato and Aristotle, along with a wide panoply of innovative thinkers, paved the way for future generations. Thanks to their efforts, the scientific disciplines were established. Artistic expression achieved a realism that glorified and thereby encouraged human ideals. Theater became more than entertainment or the transmitter of rote tradition. It channeled the wisdom, contradictions and sublime qualities of thoughtful souls. The Greek thirst for freedom instituted a longing for democracy that still inspires us, more than two millennia in the future. Other cultures now gravitate toward its benefits.

Although Greece's Classical Age eventually fell due to its lack of national unity (a lesson for all of us to learn), their love of reason and virtue continued to germinate throughout the Hellenized world, surviving centuries of war, plagues, famines and religious violence. Today, it must contend with the ubiquitous distractions of commercialism.

In the form of *Stoic philosophy*, it flourished for a while in Rome. It eventually migrated to the Persians while Europe slipped into the *Dark Ages*. Crusaders, rediscovering this knowledge in the Holy Land, carried it back to European soil, eventually igniting a flame of genius called the *Renaissance*. Progress continued in leaps and bounds during the *Age of Reason* that followed, further shaping the development of the Western mind. Mathematics and science opened the imagination to unlimited possibilities.

Despite all that progress, or maybe because of it, the tendency toward hubris continued its contagion with devastating consequences.

The power-grabbing world wars of the twentieth century traumatized the popular psyche of the West with what seemed to be the fallibility of our ideals. Who thought such atrocities were possible for a people who believed in God, human rights and the safeguards of economic interdependency? We were completely unprepared for the serpent that we had nurtured at our breasts – the serpent of nationalism, greed and discontent, agitated by exploiters of hate and paranoia. Enough was never enough.

What explanation could post-war people give to the wholesale slaughter and genocidal crimes against humanity that they themselves produced? The civilized aspects of their beliefs and self-images had been shattered. All that was left was confusion and shame.

Many chose the cowardly path. They chose not to think about it. While they could not deny what happened, they could turn their backs on it. They could ignore their own responsibility by wrapping themselves in the thoughtless conformity of the herd. People dressed more and more alike, adopted similar interests and did whatever was expected of them without question. Finding reward in material comfort, they became perfect consumers who were willingly ripe for exploitation. The entertainment industry happily propagated images that defined how people should act, what music they should like, and how they should disdain anything that was "different." The 1950s were well known for homogenizing the culture away from individuality. Either you fit in with popular expectations or you were "weird," someone to avoid, even dangerous. The challenges of the quest were pushed aside by complacently doing whatever it took to fit in.

For those who heroically continued the Western tradition of thinking for themselves, it was plain that the heart of their culture had dramatically changed into something different. The toppling of Western ideals and the mass conformity that followed had become a cultural apostasy of the worst kind. They could see that the West was losing its fundamental character. People had glimpsed the demon inside and were afraid to confront it. Unfortunately, the dull distraction of mass conformity only made things worse. People were rejecting the best part of who they were – not because it failed them, as they thought, but because *they* failed *it*.

*Existentialism* arose from this mire with a demand for personal responsibility. This austere philosophy pointed out exactly what was missing in the years that led to the obscenities of trench warfare, mustard gas, civilian bombing and genocide. Technology, greed and hubris had distracted our cultural focus away from our ideals. Existentialism made clear that the responsibilities of the individual had been misplaced. There was more to freedom than attaining economic profit at any cost – an anemic understanding of freedom that had pushed the lives of many into the hands of the few. This surrender of critical thinking is what produced two world wars and the resulting homogeneity of the masses – a state where truth receded to allow consumerism and prejudice to flourish. In the face of all that, existentialism reminded us that a person's dignity came from himself and no one else. No membership card, social status or net worth can give that to us.

People who were caught up in the false security and complacency of the herd accused existentialism of being a negative philosophy. They did not appreciate their integrity being questioned, and resented the mirror held before them. Materialism, commercialism, political bickering and a false reconstruction of historical ideals had replaced positive freedom. While the introduction of nuclear weapons brought new sobriety to our international affairs, people still found ways to shirk responsibility. The youth rebellion of the 1960s and 70s was a direct response to this. Lacking its cultural foothold, however, it threw conformity aside and introduced a new form of hedonism.

In today's world, despite all our technical skills and accumulated knowledge, the tensions between reason and ignorance, virtue and vice, responsibility and license, truth and commercial illusion, continue to flourish. A convenient yet subversive truce has been drawn to accommodate opposing values. We now pay political lip service to ideals that we scarcely follow. Material wealth, comfort and convenience have become our idols of the marketplace.

Beneath all this bartering and butchering of moral conscience, the ideals of Western civilization still managed to survive. We hold reverence for the patriotic words that are recalled on state occasions. The inspiration of our founders still rings true. We see non-Western and third world nations struggling to incorporate those ideals, which many still regard as the best great hope for humankind.

Humility reminds us that this admirable philosophy, having arisen in Western culture, is no cause for conceit. Those looking for a sense of ego-exceptionalism or feelings of racial or ethnic superiority miss the point entirely. Citizenship, association or birthright guarantees nothing in matters of honor. Only adherence to the *quest* brings with it the clarity of thought and value that supports authenticity. The results are not the possession of any group. They must be earned by each of us, one at a time.

The Roman emperor Marcus Aurelius, who exemplified Stoic philosophy, said it well:

"If the power of thought is universal among mankind, so likewise is the possession of reason, making us rational creatures. It follows, therefore, that this reason speaks no less universally to us all with its "thou shalt" and "thou shalt not." So then, there is a *world-law*, which in turn means that we are all fellow-citizens and share a common citizenship, and that the world is a single city."

The *world-law* he speaks of is also known as *Nature's Law* or *conscience*. We will consider more on that later.

More recent ethnocentrism has pushed aside this universal sentiment, which was far more enlightened than much of what we hear today. Claiming high ideals while not bothering to understand them, results in a dangerous combination of hubris and ignorance. We must never forget that if our Western ideals are true, they must have universal implications. As such, they do not *belong* to us and not to others. They are ideals that anyone can learn and benefit from.

On the other hand, even though "we believe these truths to be self-evident," we have no right to force them upon others. Force only degrades intent and invites resistance. Ideals were meant to inspire, not coerce. Anything less chokes the life from them and leads to disaster.

## Chapter 3

# Stoicism — *The Earliest Flower*

**Medieval Chivalry, which provided** the central theme in the formation of Chivalry-Now, did not appear in the Middle Ages from nowhere. Many of its ideals already had deep roots in Western culture. The earliest image of the knight appears to have been the elite cavalryman of ancient Rome and the mounted retainer of Roman aristocrats.

A powerful contributor to the warrior code of Rome was the Greek philosophy of *Stoicism*. It held that the highest virtues included justice, prudence, temperance, fortitude and detachment from wealth. Early Christians borrowed heavily from Stoicism in developing their monastic traditions.

To illustrate the similarities between Stoicism and chivalry, the words of the emperor *Marcus Aurelius* serve us well. We turn to his private collection of thoughts entitled *Meditations*, with the recommendation that you read his book in its entirety.

Despite his lineage, education, power and privilege, Marcus Aurelius was a man of simple tastes who was not given to excess. He ruled wisely and fairly. Kind and loyal to his friends, forgiving to his enemies, generous to those in need, he resembled the benevolent monarch or *philosopher king* described centuries earlier by *Plato*.

As his writings attest, he was a deeply thoughtful man who pondered the ways of nature and tried to live his life accordingly.

In *Book One* of the *Meditations*, he gives us incredible insight into the values of Stoicism by acknowledging the people who influenced him, including teachers, relatives, friends and statesmen. He carefully specified what he learned from each person. The list is quite impressive.

For sake of brevity, what follows is a transcription of those values taken from his own words. (I have italicized concepts that relate to the *12 Trusts* and Chivalry-Now.) Remember, these are the words of the most powerful man in Europe at his time. They express the very opposite of emperors with whom the media has made us more familiar, like *Caligula* and *Nero*. They list the values held by a long list of worthy people.

- *Character requires improvement and discipline.*
- The same law should be applied to all, *respecting equal rights and equal freedom of speech,* and the idea of a kingly government that strongly respects the *freedom* of the governed.
- Self-government. Not to be led aside by anything.
- *Never be a partisan.*
- Consider yourself no more than any other citizen.
- One should endure freedom of speech and become intimate with philosophy.
- Good morals and the governing of one's temper.
- *Modesty and a manly character.*
- Piety, beneficence and abstinence, not only from evil deeds, but even from evil thoughts.
- *Simplicity in one's way of living,* far removed from the habits of the rich.
- To have good teachers at home and to know that on such things people should spend liberally.
- The endurance of labor and to want little, and to work with one's own hands.
- *Not to meddle with other people's affairs and not to be ready to listen to slander.*
- Not to busy myself about trifling things and not to give credit to superstition.
- Not to be led astray by sophistry.
- *Not to show myself off as a man who practices much discipline*

*or performs benevolent acts in order to make a display.*

- With respect to those who have offended me by words or done me wrong, *to be easily disposed to be pacified and reconciled.*
- Read carefully, and not to be satisfied with a superficial understanding of a book; nor hastily give my assent to those who talk overmuch.
- Freedom of will, undeviating steadiness of purpose and *to look to nothing else, not even for a moment, except to reason.*
- The same man can be most resolute, yielding, and not peevish.
- *A benevolent disposition,* and the example of a family governed in a fatherly manner.
- *The idea of living conformably with nature.*
- *Live according to nature.*
- To tolerate ignorant persons and those who form opinions without consideration.
- Express approbation without noisy display and possess much knowledge without ostentation.
- *Refrain from fault-finding* and not in a reproachful way to chide those who speak poorly.
- Observe that envy, duplicity and hypocrisy are in a tyrant, and that generally those among us who are called patricians are rather deficient in paternal affection.
- Not to be indifferent when a friend finds fault, even if he should find fault without reason, but to try to restore him to his usual disposition.
- *Love kin, love truth and love justice.*
- Consistency and undeviating steadiness in regard to philosophy.
- *A disposition to do good, to give to others readily,* to cherish good hopes and believe that I am loved by my friends.
- Cheerfulness in all circumstances, as well as in illness.
- A just mixture in the *moral character of sweetness and dignity,*

and to do what was set before me without complaining.

- *Do acts of beneficence and be ready to forgive.*
- *Be free from all falsehood.*
- Be humorous in an agreeable way.
- Mildness of temper, unchangeable resolution, and *no vainglory in things which men call honors.*
- Love of labor and perseverance.
- A readiness to listen to those who have anything to propose for the common good.
- Give to every man according to his desserts.
- Take careful inquiry in all matters of deliberation.
- Not to be extravagant in affection.
- Be satisfied on all occasions and cheerful.
- Be wary of popular applause and all flattery.
- Take reasonable care of health.
- Do not be harsh, nor implacable, nor violent.
- Indebtedness to good family, teachers and associates.
- Never do anything that you might repent.

As one can see, Marcus Aurelius was a defender of freedom, especially free thought. He clearly saw the relationship between freedom and personal responsibility that comes from self-discipline. Judging by the list of people who influenced him, he was far from alone. This was the environment he was born into, a distinct part of our Western heritage.

It is easy to find references in Chivalry-Now that reflect this philosophy. So too Enlightenment thinking and modern existentialism – all expressions of Western thought that were influenced by Stoicism. In his recognition of equal rights and common citizenship we find the basis for our own democracy.

Most striking of all was his observation of *humility* as the proper approach to truth, which his words clearly illustrate. He also recognized the dangers that come from wealth.

We learn much from Marcus Aurelius that can be directly

applied to our own individual quests. We also gain a deeper appreciation of our cultural history. He shows that many of our ancestors were highly moral and intelligent people, sensitive to the world around them, and desirous of improving the lives of everyone.

His *Meditations* remains one of the treasures of our quest.

\* \* \*

## What does this mean for us?

Stoic philosophy laid down a noble foundation of simplicity, personal virtue, dispassionate reason and self-discipline that made possible much of Western civilization as it developed. Respect for it continued long after its ancient flourish preserving a cultural imperative that centered on truth and moral obligation. Christianity adopted much of its demeanor and asceticism. We see glaring examples of it when law is administered with impartiality and when leaders of impeccable integrity maintain their values in politics. We also see it expressed in scholarly disciplines and military establishments. Elements of Stoicism contribute in every serious endeavor by providing a foundation for ethically-minded professionalism.

We exhibit elements of Stoicism when we uphold what is right and good in the face of contention, especially when doing so risks personal sacrifice. Right action, honor and self-discipline are its mainstay. They remain the heroic qualities that form the basis of genuine self-esteem and gentlemanly behavior.

# Chapter 4

# Aletheia — *Truth*

*"Learning what is true in order to do what is right, is the summing up of the whole duty of man."*

**This quote,** attributed to *Thomas Henry Huxley,* expresses a vitally important aspect of today's chivalry. It is not enough to do what one perceives is right. *One must first determine what is right by discovering what is true.* This is what the quest is all about – learning, exploring, discovering, *and then* acting with well-earned confidence.

Most of us would agree that rational decisions are best made when supported by a strong foundation of knowledgeable truth.

In contrast, what is false naturally leads to misconceptions. Illusions distort what we perceive. Lack of curiosity, or irresponsibly adopting someone else's conclusions, sets the stage for error. Closing our minds to possibilities limits our relationship with truth, chipping away at our personal authenticity as human beings.

Because of all this, searching for truth, finding it, and incorporating it into our lives is very important. It determines right action and fulfills who we are as people. The quest we set out on is a journey into truth through which we grow and fashion ourselves according to the lessons that life brings. As a transformative process, the quest may not be perfect, but its approach is real and very human. It not only transforms, it liberates. To those who persist with an open mind, its path leads to uncommon integrity and compassion, which is the height of human development.

Unfortunately, as a concept, truth can be difficult to grasp.

Our limited minds cannot encompass it entirely. We can find bits and pieces as we journey on our quest, or corral a lifetime of facts and reasonable assumptions into an integrated blend of wisdom. Nevertheless, the grand scope of truth escapes us. Huge tracts appear completely incomprehensible. In a way, we are like computers. We can only save and integrate what is compatible with our mental programming. We can utilize only what we can recognize.

The theologian Paul Tillich pointed out something grander, a reality with universal implications. He referred to it as *ultimate truth*, which by nature had to be *all inclusive*. If something exists, it partakes in this truth by necessity. As living beings we are part of it. Thanks to our conscious minds, we not only partake in truth, we are capable of relating to it.

Seen from this perspective, truth is not limited to dealing with accumulated facts. It provides a vital dimension to our very existence.

To better understand this, we turn to the ancients for what insight they provide. People of the distant past were closer to nature than we are today. Their encounter with truth was uniquely fresh and more intuitive. While not always correct in their assumptions, their thoughts are often quite revealing.

Greek philosophers referred to truth as *Aletheia* (a-LEE-thē-a). The rich etymology of this word offers us incredible insights that would otherwise be lost. As the quest helps us rediscover our cultural inheritance, we do well to reclaim them.

The root meanings of Aletheia are as follows:

1   Not being hidden.
2   Remembering (or recognizing).
3   A not-death-experience (or life-expanding).

These concepts inform us that we should not approach truth as if it were a commodity, something outside us that we can physically grasp (although mythical symbolism often portrayed it as such). If truth is all-encompassing and we are part of it, then this denial of separation makes perfect sense.

Truth exists. It is what is, whether we recognize it or not. When we *discover* it, we are not finding something that was lost or previously nonexistent. We acknowledge that it is *no longer hidden* by our lack of perception. We *recognize* the self-evident quality of truth as it expands our consciousness of what is. We integrate it with what we already hold in memory, which can be likened to *remembering*. This is especially true when it awakens innate properties of our minds, such as conscience or spiritual awe.

When we consider Aletheia as a *not-death-experience,* we learn that a proper relationship with truth profoundly adds to our experience of the moment. It is *life-expanding*. We feel this most directly while learning something that interests us. Inspiration fuels and ignites our energy. We feel more complete. Learning enraptures us with excitement – not just by incorporating individual facts, but with their depth of meaning. We become more open and engaged.

This is especially true when we include a recognition of Mystery as well. Mystery allows us to include what we cannot comprehend. It validates necessary gaps in knowledge while enticing us to learn more.

Honest investigation allows Mystery to be part of the equation – the *x-factor* if you will. The paradoxical nature of existence calls for that. To reference this unknown, we often use words like *spiritual* or *mystical.* We separate it from science in order to protect the integrity of both.

\* \* \*

**There have always been exceptional people** who have sacrificed their lives in order to protect or promote some grand concept of truth. There have also been those who allowed ignorance to lead them into war or persecution. Our relationship with truth can be that decisive.

For most of us, truth can be found just about anywhere, in the simple quiet of a colorful sunset or in the paradoxical observations of quantum mechanics. It is sometimes equated with God. To the philosopher, it can mean the all-inclusive reality that we struggle to understand.

Aletheia tells us that truth is a vital ingredient in our maturation process – not just as the folly of youth struggles to transform itself into the wisdom of maturity, but in the extension of consciousness as well. The mind that continues to learn, that contemplates truth, and develops its own virtues in the process, experiences more of life than someone who thoughtlessly stagnates in a confined repetition of daily routine. There is a lack of authenticity in someone who is constantly shaped by the thoughts and values of others. It is a sign of broken autonomy, a loss of personhood.

We are born into the world with varying degrees of potential, including a measure of conscience that helps shape our moral development. Family, religion, society and the commercial media influence that development. Such factors, accompanied by varying degrees of social pressure, are often more upfront and demanding than that quiet inner voice that nags us when something is wrong. When we adopt the values and opinions of others we must, to some extent, disregard not only conscience but our natural curiosity as well. We seldom even question the surrender of this responsibility. By following the crowd, or a particular leader or ideology, we forego the autonomy that conscience makes possible. Our moral decisions, instead of being carefully thought out, are decided by herd instinct, colloquial folk wisdom, thoughtless clichés and superstition. What we call the *law of the jungle*, little more than a convenient excuse to exploit others, tramples on moral reasoning that took millennia to develop.

We see the results everywhere. Endemic greed, once condemned as one of the seven deadly sins, has infiltrated just about every aspect of our society, from business to politics to religion. We see it openly propagated in schools, in sports, in relationships, and never-ending international tensions.

Greed is portrayed as something good, as something attractive, even manly in a perverse sort of way. Our economy has so grown to depend on it that we tend to think of capitalism more as a national philosophy rather than an economic system that can be used for good or ill.

Greed has long been condemned by every legitimate religion. While we may enjoy its many addictive aspects – the conveniences, diversions and status symbols – we must remind ourselves that a greed-centric life does not allow our internal well-being to flourish. Authenticity comes not from possessions or bank accounts, but from *aspirations of consciousness*. The trappings of wealth easily become distractions from authentic living. This set of values, equated with material success, then filters out to the general public. People envy what they do not have, increasing their appetites to the point where meaningful fulfillment no longer matters.

From a quest perspective, something of our humanity is lost in this process.

When religious leaders degrade eternal truths for the sake of television ratings, an important cultural paradigm has drastically shifted away from truth. When politicians measure their words according to fear and regional bias, democracy, which depends upon intelligence and honesty, begins its fatal descent. When business leaders ruin their own companies in order to reap huge bonuses, the economy, and civilization along with it, loses its integrity and tilts toward collapse.

Conservatives throw truth out the window by telling us not to trust human reason, the very quality that defines us and is responsible for our success. Notice how they treat the latest scientific warnings about the environment with scorn. Liberals promote selected versions of partial truths without relating them to the whole, trying to fix this problem or that as if the myriad factors contributing to them could be ignored. For example, welfare does not end poverty. It sustains it. One of these ideologies resists all change, no matter how vital, while the other lobbies for surface-level change that continually misses the mark.

With profit-based media encouragement, the two battle each other without scruples, convincing the gullible that there are only two world views to choose from. Intuitively, most people understand this as an assault upon their intelligence and ignore them both, allowing the travesty to continue. Despite the minority status of extremism, we remain subjected to the cyclical rise and fall of their policies that make a farce of our Western ideals.

In the meantime, disconnected from this farce as much as possible, most of us do our best to live reasonably decent lives. We raise our families, obey the laws, work for a living, enjoy free time – and repress our fundamental discouragement deep inside.

The message of Aletheia reminds us that truth is more than a momentary distraction. Our lives need not be small and transitory, given to meaningless chatter, long lines and cheap diversions. At any moment, *this moment especially*, we can follow our deeper quests and reclaim our true nobility.

Aletheia shows us how.

* * *

**Truth is a transformational** experience because knowledge instigates personal change.

When one fully understands a threat, one will prudently take precautions to avoid it. Nothing could be more obvious and sensible. Knowing more about the world we live in contributes to the transformation of adolescence into adulthood.

But our insight into Aletheia suggests more than that. Jesus told us that *the truth would set us free*. Adequate moral understanding, and the responsibility that comes with it, bequeaths a type of moral autonomy that liberates us from ignorance and the slavery imposed by other people's expectations. We become more complete persons. Such transformation should concern us all as a requirement for personal growth.

Sometimes we react to the discovery of truth with personal change that is immediate and quite profound. Like a splash of reality that awakens us from the slumbering values of our dull routines, our whole perspective suddenly changes.

The awakening of who we are, and *who we can be*, is no small thing. Everything in our lives is contingent upon our own self-perception. Engaging life with new intensity and awareness can be likened to a second birth.

Not surprisingly, the Greeks had a word for it. They called it *anagnorisis* (ah-nog-NOR-isis), a sudden insight that changes one's perception not only of the world but of oneself. It is a moment when the realization of truth changes our whole view of reality.

In Greek drama, anagnorisis represented the moment when the hero responds in life-transforming ways to facts that were previously hidden. *Aristotle*, in his *Poetics*, considered this revelation to be an essential element of tragedy. This is dramatically illustrated in *Oedipus Rex*, when the main character learned the happenstance of his birth. His view of the world and the role he played changed completely.

Moving away from its theatrical application, anagnorisis can be viewed as a transformational awakening of our moral centers that completes who we are. It is the obtainable fruit of self-development that comes from living life as a quest.

For Chivalry-Now, anagnorisis is the moment when truth significantly awakens us to the living moment with all its moral imperatives and we respond accordingly. It is consciousness activated in the here and now, bringing us into a closer, more fundamental relationship with truth. This awareness makes us more alive.

Anagnorisis opens our eyes to those dimensions of truth that we previously failed to appreciate because they were *hidden* from our perceptions. No longer hidden, Aletheia strips away the illusions that previously misled us. We may find ourselves on the same path, but our perspective is very different.

What inhibits this rebirth of the soul is a culture that no longer values its deeper qualities – a culture that systematically cajoles us to place reason and wholesome curiosity aside and surrender to illusion. We disengage our powers of discernment in order to fit in. We ignore Mystery by convincing ourselves that the marketplace, of all things most superficial, and purposely so, provides all the answers that we need. In a world that caters to illusion, truth loses its relevance. The lies and fantasy that replace it leave us with a discontent that is endemic.

In this society, we habitually contend with the opposite of Aletheia: falsehood, deception, a state of not knowing who we are, confining our lives to something small and frustratingly inauthentic. After billions of years of evolution, the miracle of human life that each of us encapsulates, capable of understanding and contributing to the good of all, simply refuses to comply with our altruistic potential. We become fallen miracles, tragically wasted.

*The quest* provides a remedy to that fate.

\* \* \*

**For some of us,** our first encounter with chivalry is derived from an encounter with Aletheia that immediately sparks a transformational experience. Something stirs inside us with recognition – the awakening of a hero that has long yearned to come alive. It beckons with the promise of personal completeness. In that very moment, our values change. Everyday distractions become meaningless in comparison. This is anagnorisis.

The words, ideals and symbols of chivalry resonate from a thousand generations past in ways that are relevant to the here and now. We instinctively know that we have stumbled upon our real inheritance, the legacy of humanity's noblest aspirations. When we grasp that connection and claim it as our own, the threshold is crossed.

The quest takes on new meaning. It projects a purpose that transcends personal growth. The *12 Trusts* are no longer a code or list of words to follow or by which to be inspired. They express that portion of Aletheia that pulsates in our hearts.

\* \* \*

### What does this mean for us?

If we ever hope to restore the energy and inspiration of Western ideals, which have steadily declined for almost two centuries, we need to start at the beginning. As individuals, we need to reconstruct our own relationship with truth. Without that foundation, everything else is make-believe, an illusion – more precisely, *a lie*. The ancient Greeks understood this. So began their world-changing quest for reason that brought new light to humanity. The capacity for reason, which defines who we are as a species, depends on truth in order to function properly. Without truth, reason turns us into fools and leads us to ruin.

Truth is more than a collection of facts. For human beings, it is a relationship with the world from which authenticity is derived. Truth brings nobility to life. It is powerful. Exciting. Inspirational. Because we are part of truth, it reveals who we are. It brings new values to life, freeing us from the shackles of ignorance while elevating humanity.

Our subjective experience of Aletheia carries meanings that are quite profound. They suggest that truth is not something to be found outside us, but something we are part of already. We relate to it when it is no longer hidden from our consciousness. Truth is so intrinsically part of who we are that discovering it is similar to *remembering*. Aletheia shows that a positive relationship with truth resonates with great energy and awareness. It is life-expanding, or as the Greeks put it, a *not-death-experience*.

Our attitude toward truth changes over the years. I have witnessed this in my own life. When I was a child, the world I encountered was explained to me by adults. For the most part, I took their word as fact, even when I could not understand them completely. Everywhere I turned I saw authority figures who could be trusted. Back then, radio and television provided news that was very different from today. They informed us about what was happening in the world, rather than titillating our baser instincts with gossip and political propaganda. Did it have a liberal slant? I believe it did. Back then, liberalism was not a dirty word. It suggested living up to our Western ideals, including freedom, civil liberties and equal rights, which are the corner-stones of Western ideals. Conservatism performed the role of safeguarding traditions while slowing down progress for the sake of cultural acclimation.

All this changed as extremists discovered that they could raise a following by carrying their strategies to the absurd. Truth was the first virtue to fall, along with civility and concern for others. Patriotism was steered away from the good of the people. Honesty was replaced by the political expediency of generating fear and distrust. When enemies are imagined everywhere, individuality becomes suspect and the essence of freedom is lost.

We are now at the point in this topsy-turvy world where truth is so compromised that it is unable to countermand outright lies. Too many people, brainwashed by lies and paranoia, are simply not interested in discovering what is true and what is not. They prefer to manufacture their own realities in support of their biases, and refuse to move beyond them.

Politicians who encourage and exploit this problem play with fire. When patriotism is invoked to destroy our finest ideals, it becomes monstrous, a degenerative process through which we destroy ourselves, while power-hungry leaders rake in the profits. We will look more into politics later on.

## Chapter 5

# Areté — *The Highest Virtue*

**The parameters of language influence** the culture that expresses it. The use and imagery of words, with their subtle meanings, configure responses in the neural conductors of the brain where they instigate thought and shape our understanding of the world.

Words represent fact and substance, but also nuance and allusion. They express emotion. They can inspire people or subject them to boredom. Beauty, coarseness, mediocrity, ignorance and genius all find expression in the use of language.

There is no calculating the fate of a culture for want of a specific word, such as God or freedom or truth. Would justice exist in a world where the concept was never spoken? Would other references compensate? What if they did not?

We have difficulty thinking of things that have no word to represent them. We would probably not consider them at all. Likewise, the introduction of a new word or concept that carries significant meaning might change our outlook on everything.

What would happen if we had a word in our vocabulary that represented the *highest virtue*, or the *greatest good*, as it applies to the excellent functioning of human nature and the reasoning mind? If this concept were well-articulated and understood by all, it would surely influence what it means to be human by providing an example or goal. As people rose to meet that expectation, the culture itself would benefit and further propagate its meaning.

Such a word would encourage concepts of personal integrity, eradicate superstition, and elevate society according to the achievements of virtue and reason. Think of how differently we would relate to one other, and how we would view ourselves.

There is such a word.

Its inspiration once contributed to the explosion of creativity and intellectual accomplishments of Western civilization's Golden Age. Doing so, it built the foundation for who we are as a people and still remains in our collective memory, largely unarticulated and unappreciated.

The word is *Areté* (AH-rē-tay), meaning *the greatest good* or *highest virtue*. Within the constellation of Chivalry-Now's Esoterica, it holds a key place of honor and distinction.

The influence of Greek philosophy has always been a powerful force in the development of Western civilization. This is especially true in areas such as freedom, individuality, logic, science, democracy, art, and so much more. Socrates, Plato and Aristotle, along with many others, form our earliest luminaries of renown.

Unfortunately, much of what we inherited has been tarnished by the vagrancies of time. Our present culture is very different from that of ancient Greece. So is our understanding of the world.

Part of that difference has to do with language. The Greek idiom offers a rich vocabulary filled with subtlety and distinction. Many of its words have no counterpart in modern European languages, relegating much of their wisdom beyond our normal intellectual purview.

*Areté* is one of those words, one that provides an important prerequisite for the understanding of freedom. It points out, for example, that virtue and reason can only flourish in a state of freedom. This is what gives freedom its intrinsic value and purpose.

The purpose of freedom is to make the greatest good possible. It facilitates reason. Virtue loses its meaning if it is forced and not freely chosen and expressed. Nothing is more repulsive than freedom when it is misused.

The founders of the United States, in their efforts to form a government based on liberty and citizen involvement, felt no need to elaborate on virtue and reason as the natural basis for their republic. They considered it self-evident and therefore plainly known by all. Reason and virtue were much talked about in the intellectual milieu of the 18$^{th}$ century, thanks to contemporary European philosophers of what was later called the Age of Enlightenment. This is where the inspiration of forming a new kind of government came from. The Declaration of Independence, Constitution and Bill of Rights reflected this in no uncertain terms.

Philosophically, Areté refers to the excellent performance of the *unique characteristics* for which a thing or species is recognized. For a bird it might be flying. For a horse, running. A firefly, how brightly it glows.

For human beings, the *rational and virtuous mind* proves to be our highest, distinguishing attribute as a species. We succeed as individuals when we excel in reason and virtue.

It seemed obvious to the ancient Greeks that intellect and virtuous compassion define what is unique in human nature. These are the qualities that humanity naturally aspires to. Areté is achieved when these attributes *function excellently*. Quite simply, when a person masters rational thinking and the moral-discipline that right living demands, he or she expresses the Areté of who we really are.

Human Areté completes us as human beings. A climate of freedom facilitates its achievement. Likewise, we cannot truly be free without first becoming who and what we really are as rational, moral beings. Without that prerequisite, freedom becomes an amoral commodity, without purpose or direction.

This is important to understand.

To be *free human beings* we must be *human beings* first, in the full sense of the word. Areté shows us how to achieve that through a marriage of reason and virtue. Anything less would produce the freedom of a domesticated cow, wandering without direction or concern. More is expected of human freedom because *reason and virtue are what make us human.*

If we disregard this, as we often do, freedom becomes an excuse for exploitation, crime, corruption and all sorts of immoral behavior. Law becomes an inconvenience. Love loses its compassion. Exploitation of others becomes acceptable and commonplace.

\* \* \*

**There is no easy translation** of Areté into English. While it is often translated as *the greatest good* or *highest virtue,* this falls short of its full significance. For human beings, the greatest good depends upon our capacity for attending the moment with clarity of thought and vision, in conjunction with conscience and compassion. Thought, logic, moral reasoning and a high level of consciousness are what separate us from other creatures. They account for our many advantages, our technologies, our laws and social contracts, and our relationships – complicated as they are.

The reasoning mind confronts virtue in the form of *conscience,* also known as *Nature's Law.* We find this deeply rooted in ourselves in the construct of familial love, friendship, patriotism, philanthropy, and compassion. All these expressions of human nature gain levels of excellence when combined with reason. We are only complete when reason and virtue function harmoniously as a structural whole.

Ancient philosophers expounded the concept of Areté to their audiences and influenced people accordingly. People became inspired to do their best in everything. This resulted in the remarkable accomplishments of the Golden Age of classical Greece which, in less than two centuries, constructed the blueprint for Western civilization. A significant portion of who we are traces back to a handful of city-states where people sought to achieve their own Areté.

We could use such inspiration now.

The Renaissance produced a resurgence of these classical ideals. A tide of geniuses transformed Dark Age Europe into an exciting era of progress and light. This movement went on to produce the Age of Reason and Enlightenment.

We see this progressive tide of reason and virtue ebb and flow throughout the history of the West, presenting the vast potential of human nature in contrasting extremes. When it flows, we reap incredible benefits of authenticity, both in quality and grandeur. When it ebbs, we become small, closed-minded, violent and destructive.

It is here, in these contradictory choices, where our spiritual nobility either lives or dies. Bloodlines, titles and wealth mean nothing compared to what values blossom inside us. We either contribute to the greater good with who we are, or we detract from it.

Which choice delivers more promise and abundant life? Which better completes who we really are?

\* \* \*

**We cannot adequately relate to truth**, to *Aletheia*, without the kind of activated reason and virtue that *Areté* prescribes. Without that personal involvement, our quest for chivalry is nothing more than an empty suit of armor, or *Don Quixote's* sad, nostalgic dream. Areté makes it possible for us to change that. Aletheia provides our quest with direction and lessons to be learned.

The personal growth that Areté represents comes from an evolution of perspective, an openness to truth and learning that makes the benefits of the quest possible. Our daily encounters and challenges, big and small, become learning opportunities that unveil and fortify who we are. This relationship with truth encourages self-discipline and self-development. *Only when a certain level of Areté is achieved are the qualities we are looking for truly born.*

We are then obligated to repair the culture in which we live – not according to some personality, cult or political ideology, but through the direct inspiration of Aletheia as we encounter it with open minds. Areté gives us the power and ability to do that.

Understanding and utilizing the word Areté opens new possibilities for growth and understanding. It focuses on a natural progression of human nature that adds significance to our relationship with the world and those with whom we share it. We can envision the excellent achievement of reason and virtue that today's knighthood can offer. When we inspire others to do likewise, we transform our world for the better – not through rules and regulations, but through the dynamics of freedom and responsibility.

Areté is nature's impetus for progress and cultural improvement. It preserves what is best of what came before us while allowing progress its proper due.

Chivalry-Now points to the importance of Areté in its *1st Trust: I will develop my life for the greater good.* It does not shape us from the outside. We are called upon to evolve from within as part of our quest.

It begins with *consciousness*, the living awareness that gives birth to the rational mind and awareness of virtue, and to the desire for self-improvement, compassion, and service to others. *Responsible consciousness* is the foundation of authenticity, integrity and personal freedom. It provides the heart with moral justice and self-reflection. All of this comes from a direct experience of life itself, and can never be imposed by others.

Chivalry-Now believes in the human potential that Areté unveils – potential to think for ourselves, question stale beliefs, and do what is right. Here we find the truest, quickest, most cost-effective approach to social improvement and personal fulfillment.

Esoterica, the collection of concepts that form the basis for Chivalry-Now, tells us to make Areté part of our vocabulary so that others might hear, question and learn, and measure themselves accordingly.

This in itself is a powerful step to heal our culture and instigate much needed change.

# Chapter 6

# Telos—*Inner Aim*

**Consciousness and reason,** while essential to our success and survival as a species, certainly add complicated burdens to our finite lives.

For one thing, we are stricken by the knowledge of our own mortality. It does not seem right that such a priceless phenomenon as human consciousness, with its powers of discernment, reflection and memory, should come into the world only to pass away. Religions talk about eternal life in another world, or reincarnation, but even that fails to sooth our anxiety. Such amazing gifts of consciousness, bordering on the miraculous, should enjoy more significance and permanence than merely the measurement of consumption, reproduction, trials and labor, all dissipated by the inevitability of death.

Our psychic balance sheet does not sit well with this. Its absurdity forms one of the unconscious frustrations that many of us carry. We hate to even think of it.

To shed light on this, we introduce another concept dating back to ancient Greece. *Telos*. Its inclusion in Esoterica provides a realistic approach to finding purpose and meaning in our finite lives. Respecting the principles of the quest, it continues to place the onus of discovery on the individual.

The word Telos can be translated as *goal* or *inner aim* which, in itself, suggests purpose and meaning.

One might describe Telos as an intent that emanates from one's own being that determines what one becomes – something like fate or destiny, yet different as well. Telos is the inner drive to realize one's own potential – a spontaneous will or urge to transform and to *become*.

That a zygote becomes a fetus, which then becomes a baby who grows into a child, and then an adult, provides a clear example of Telos expressed physically – what we now recognize as the workings of genetics. Physical growth and maturity happen on their own when a reasonable amount of health and safety are maintained.

Poetically speaking, one might describe the fertilized embryo as carrying the *destiny* of a fully actualized adult who will someday become a responsible citizen. Although ancient philosophers knew nothing about DNA, their assumptions described what today's genetic sciences fully recognize as a mechanistic function. Inner goals seek to be realized. The blueprint for maturation is embedded in a physical code – that actualizes itself.

Is there a spiritual or moral code as well? Do the *12 Trusts* articulate them?

For Chivalry-Now, the principle of Telos refers to an inner aim or personal drive *to realize one's own potential*. It is life fulfilling its own *self-generated goals,* no matter how hidden or unconsciously initiated. Each of us carries an inner aim that ultimately defines who we are.

Of course, the realization of our potential can certainly be interrupted or diverted. Not all children survive to adulthood. A person's DNA might be faulty. Disease might strike. Miscarriages happen. Innocent people have their lives cut short by war, famine or a thousand other reasons. Death eventually takes us all.

When a person achieves a long and fruitful life, we think of that life as being fulfilled. Telos reached its completion.

This is not to say that outside influences are not involved. Family certainly comes to bear on early childhood development and beyond. Friends, teachers, mentors, cultural values and economic status also leave indelible marks. As one matures, this includes spouses, business acquaintances, and parental responsibilities toward children. Health and happenstance are certainly part of the equation. So are the choices we make that steer us in various directions.

Beneath all that complexity, however, is the functional instinct of our inner aim, that part of our nature which carries its own tendencies toward growth. DNA is part of it, of course – perhaps all of it at some level. Unfortunately, our understanding of DNA is limited. It does not account for such intangibles as instinct, intuition, archetypal tendencies, and so forth. It does not account for the quasi-spiritual experience of consciousness, or for the moral tendencies that we regard as humane, or the nobility of one's character. A unique mixture of nature and nurture contributes to the making of each person's individuality.

Telos might be described as that part of us that springs from nature rather than nurture in deciding our development.

Hitler was not produced in a vacuum. He was the result of inner potentials that were influenced by family, culture and historical events. Hindsight might conclude that his life fulfilled a prearranged destiny, but that would be misleading. For all we know, there may have been hundreds of potential Hitlers who never succeeded in manifesting their maniacal intent. We can be thankful for that.

Likewise, there are many exceptionally good people who never achieve the accomplishments of Gandhi. It does not make them any less good.

Each of us has potential. Each of us experiences variables in life through which that potential is shaped, guided and allowed to express itself. Disregarding outside influences, which can be powerful, the inner drive that shapes our potential is what we call Telos.

Understanding Telos is important in that it allows us to peek into our original nature to find the tendencies of developmental personhood before outside factors intervene.

\* \* \*

**The value of Telos is simple.** If one is aware of nature's inner aim, one can consciously participate in its fulfillment. Since this inner aim is part of who we are, and provides the direction toward who we should be, a serious approach to life should take this into account.

When we think of virtue as something outside us, something that makes personal demands, or contradicts our narrow views of freedom and self-interest, our relationship to virtue is less than optimum. From this perspective, duality abounds, and conflicting values become the norm.

Telos promotes something far more functional. It recognizes that we are beings who are constantly in a transitional state, complete in who we are, yet not as complete as we will be as our potential is fulfilled.

This is especially true in regard to virtue. The process of real growth aims toward greater and greater authenticity. We become more human as we become more humane. Virtue and nobility are part of that. As thinking, judging, feeling creatures, virtue is a vital part of our authenticity (our Areté). It blossoms from within as a human construct. (In contrast, moral inclinations are meaningless to a rock or tree.) If it were imposed from outside, or even perceived that way, it would be artificial, incomplete, difficult to sustain. It would create a façade rather than feed the inner drive that promotes our true identity.

Duality, with all of its mystical baggage, becomes an illusion that no longer makes sense. Positive values naturally coalesce when uninterrupted, igniting the excitement of freedom with a more profound depth of purpose and meaning.

All this is facilitated when we become conscious of our own personal Telos, our internal prompting for growth and development. It awakens who we are deep inside and carries our quest to a higher level. At some point in our journey, if all goes well, a hero is born, a hero defined by qualities derived from virtue.

The quest takes on new meaning. In the early stages, it

concentrates on personal growth and consciousness. Once a sufficient degree of authenticity is attained, preparation leads to action. The quest opens up from a self-contained journey to greater-inclusiveness, which is what the hero's purpose is all about. It relates to the world and unleashes a prepared individual who valiantly contributes to the greater good.

Of course we continue to learn and grow as our quests continue. The difference is that we transform from being students in preparation, to protagonists capable of effective action.

This is how the inner aim of Telos leads us to personal fulfillment, validated by a thousand mythical stories and by what each of us knows inherently, if we listen to our conscience. *Telos makes us yearn for our own nobility* – the acquisition of which, unlike physical growth, is a conscious decision. Telos gently pushes us to develop our heroic qualities, which leads to fulfillment. The quest provides the means to achieve that goal.

We can resist, of course. Many of us do. A society filled with noisy distractions, conflicting values and amoral sophistry encourages just that. With little or no cultural guidance taking the lead, we must make a concerted effort to promote our own natural development. We must seek to purposely regain our moral inheritance.

As individuals, we need to recognize, nurture, and give precedence to our moral strivings. Knowing that Telos is at work in each of us, and that its goal is to fulfill who we are as valuable citizens of the world, immediately gives life to new perspectives. The nostalgia we feel when confronting chivalry is a direct result of the instinctive yearning we have for a culture that honors and supports the nobility of human nature. It calls us to reject the moral infancy that society caters to. Our latent hero, the best part of who we are, wants to live.

Hence the appeal of Chivalry-Now to people of conscience.

\* \* \*

**Just as we are capable** of choosing right from wrong, we choose who we are as well.

While personal change is often difficult, we can draw strength from tendencies that are already inside us, longing for fulfillment. We need to embrace them and change will follow. Telos reflects the goals of nature. There is nothing artificial about it.

As rational creatures, we can facilitate this process. To an extent, we can better choose what books to read, the people we associate with, what career to follow. We can educate ourselves toward freedom of the mind and resist constraining ideologies. We can turn away from things that impede growth, such as chemical addiction or worthless distractions that seduce our minds from moving forward.

We can reevaluate the surrounding variables that would control us, such as family expectations, peer pressure, politics, charismatic personalities, habit, and pervasive commercialism. We can set them aside if we want. It may be difficult, but attaining the purpose of our lives is no small responsibility.

The knight of legend was motivated by a desire to exemplify certain ideals. He did this through personal commitment, the development of certain skills, and behavior meant to shape his destiny.

His commitment to chivalry and the quest influenced his everyday behavior. Was this the result of outside influences? To a certain extent, it was. Back then, the culture encouraged such ideals, supporting his personal Telos. Society made a point of propagating its own moral well-being.

None of us are in the godlike position of being able to shape our environment completely to our liking. We are surrounded by competing interests and the complexities that they bring. Unlike the knight of old, we hear little that encourages us to seek truth, honor, virtue, or to develop our lives for the greater good. Our culture fails us in this. Much of what we hear points in the opposite direction.

Even so, we can work toward goals of our own choosing and honor principles that steer us toward better results. We might not achieve them, but our chances increase significantly when we do more than sit back and complain.

Writing a book on Chivalry-Now was the goal of a lifetime for me. It was never guaranteed that I would get it finished. Literary agents told me that I would never find an interested publisher. For many disappointing years they seemed to be right. The market was far more interested in formula fiction and scandal than a treatise on virtue.

The book eventually got published. It would not have happened if I had quit a day sooner. I persevered because I believed in what I was doing. When prospects looked bleak and frustration took hold, I would step back, return to study, and allow the project's rationale to build in my mind. My wife and members of our fellowship encouraged me to continue. With every delay, the concepts I wrote about became more real and the manuscript improved.

I believe it was my personal Telos that drove me to continue.

\* \* \*

**Many of us experience** a strong simpatico with chivalric ideals from the moment we first hear about them. The principles so resonate in our conscience that they seem to be ours already. We experience a feeling of connection, even ownership. Words that many consider passé, like truth, justice, honor and courtesy, suddenly ring with new significance and inspiration.

Today's society considers such ideals outdated. They contend, after all, with amoral consumerism. Some people actually feel threatened by them. If individuals suddenly awoke from their consumerist mentality, social values would have to change to something that supports virtue. Profiting from vice and duplicity would no longer be acceptable. I doubt that the marketing community would welcome such a change.

What marketers fail to realize (along with politicians and pundits and media personalities) is that the tenets of chivalry still hold significant reference within our collective memory. When accessed, they make it clear that some values are simply better, truer and more humane than others. Despite all the madness, we remain innately attached to chivalry's ideals.

I suggest, therefore, that chivalry is not dead. It is merely asleep. All we need do is awaken it.

*Consider:*

- We still admire the self-discipline of gentlemanly behavior associated with this code of ethics.
- We recognize that those who are adept at reason, compassion and courtesy seem more complete, more authentic, and more trustworthy than those who are not.
- We value people of character, and intuitively admire the true hero.
- Just as intuitively, we feel repulsed by cowardice.
- Conscience still pricks us with indignation while witnessing unfairness.
- We appreciate courtesy when it is extended and usually feel drawn to reciprocate.
- We expect people to tell the truth, and resent it when they do not.
- We still hold justice as a central theme of the social contract.

These inclinations are part of our nature, whether innate, gleaned from culture, or both.

Western civilization still provides tantalizing glimpses of

chivalry in literature and film, just enough to retain our connection with it. From episodes of the *Lone Ranger* to the more recent trilogy, *Lord of the Rings,* its lure remains epic in proportion. Through fact and fiction, chivalry provides a conduit to our cultural inheritance from the distant past. There are other sources as well, including military and civic organizations, scouting, reenactment groups, and certain family, community and religious traditions. Each preserves bits and pieces of our ideals for future generations. This is why chivalry still provokes a sense of moral nostalgia whenever we find it.

* * *

**Does Telos suggest** that chivalric principles are innate in the human psyche?

Here we must tread lightly. As tantalizing as the prospect may be, it is difficult to know. Nevertheless, the idea that these perennial ideals are intrinsically part of who we are remains enticing. For one thing, it suggests *an inherent nobility in human nature* that might not otherwise be there.

Telos suggests that human nature is not as shallow as consumerism would make it. It becomes shallow through a process of indoctrination, and may be far richer and more profound than anyone ever guessed. Perhaps our social problems are not so much a curse but a warning that we have strayed from our own evolution. The problems will worsen until we reclaim the moral dignity that we lost.

Telos suggests that humanity is basically good. This certainly places more value on human life than the opposite conclusion. Coming from the perspective that people are fundamentally bad makes excuses for bad behavior. When we then focus on modifying behavior through reward and punishment, or coercion, we fail to nourish the value of morality for morality's sake. We lessen personal esteem and equate moral resolve with something that is unnatural. Trust also comes into question. Mercy becomes expendable. The downtrodden are automatically slighted for lack of discipline. We distrust our own motives, and look to authoritative leaders for affirmation.

But who are these leaders? Why should they be any better than the rest of us? And what happens when we surrender our autonomy? Do we not lose our moral integrity in the process?

Even if we reject the idea that virtues are innate, that does not prove that people are inherently bad. The newborn child seems neither good nor bad. Whatever tendencies she displays in the future may be determined by what she learns. One recalls John Locke's *tabula rasa*, or blank slate, waiting to be filled. Why assume that such a child is automatically sinful?

The truth is that most people do not make such assumptions about newborn children. We instinctively know better. Arguments to the contrary are artificially imposed.

We are creatures shaped by our own beliefs, be they scientific, religious, personal, cultural, or all of the above. We need to examine those beliefs to see if they are reasonable and produce good results.

Whether or not our ideals are at least partially innate may not be as important as believing that they are. Throughout history, myth, folklore and religion have led us to believe that we can improve ourselves through an experiential learning process called the quest. Where did the continuity of that message come from? The answer is simple. Deep inside our subconscious, we know it is true.

We may never be able to prove that elements of chivalry are innate with scientific certainty. But then, there is no real need. The quest shows us, through activated conscience, that there is something in human nature that gravitates toward virtue, no matter how we are distracted or pulled in other directions. We recognize its value, admire its demonstration, and honor those who exemplify it. We go so far as to create imaginary heroes out of villains just to satisfy our need for someone virtuous to emulate.

This is Telos at work. We are more authentic because of it.

Consider how we easily conclude that something is *wrong* with people who behave poorly or lack a sense of conscience. We consider them abnormal, deviant, or at least victims of poor upbringing.

Personality problems stand out despite all the conflicting values that surround us. Some of these influences would convince us that selfishness and greed are forces for good. Even when capitalism runs amok, our lives seem to benefit – food is more plentiful and affordable. Technological innovations remain constant. Medical science accomplishes wonders that keep more and more people alive and healthy.

None of that can be denied. But is that where our concerns should end? Our bellies may be full, our phones more convenient, our blood pressures artificially lowered – and all that is good and beneficial – but what of the viability of our souls?

Some say that risk is the unavoidable cost of freedom. Is that true? Has the risk of freedom become the most likely cause of spiritual stagnation?

If it has, then freedom has lost its most enriching and ennobling features. Rather than the surest path to authentic living, it is rapidly becoming something amoral and uninspiring.

We make a terrible mistake when we assume that freedom, as a Western ideal, is an end unto itself. It is a *means to an end*. Its purpose is to make good things possible, chief among them being personal growth. It is the means through which human goodness finds the authenticity to express itself.

If freedom does not produce positive results, it can easily produce a self-concept that is faltering or incomplete or inhumane, or one that drifts away from our moral centers instead of bringing them to life. In contrast, the hallmark of freedom is its potential to give us purpose and meaning that completes who we are and benefits the world in the process.

Unfortunately, our present day culture, which thrives on selfishness, no longer focuses on that.

\* \* \*

**Telos can be likened to an inner yearning** that draws us toward what is good.

For the most part, Western culture does not consider good and evil as equal forces, or suggest that the balance of the two is somehow essential to the ways of the universe. It denies that good and evil are two sides of the same coin; that they are opposites opposed to one another could not be more plain. When one gains ground, the other often recedes.

Good does not need evil in order to exist. If it did, the *quantitative* relationship between them would be constant. No person or society would be better or worse than another. No act could claim the moral high ground. The balance would show a fixed symbiosis everywhere we look, which would ultimately rob virtue of its meaning and life of its purpose and direction.

Does it make sense to say that we need more vice in order to promote more virtue? Does totalitarianism bring as much benefit to people's lives as a democracy? Do lies produce more truth? Do ignorance and superstition foster reason and intelligence? Does the good of the few excuse the misery of the many?

We cannot justify the existence of evil in the name of freedom or goodness without relinquishing our moral integrity. When we equate freedom with the law of the jungle, the most laudable aspects of human nature are maligned.

Our inner Telos pushes us to become people who do what is right. It is that indispensable urge that makes the quest a birthing process through which authenticity is born and purposeful freedom finds its value.

Culture is supposed to facilitate that process. Its purpose is to give us not only direction, but the moral and intellectual tools to help us grow beyond our baser instincts. It is our link to the past, the storeroom of wisdom upon which we build.

Culture should make plain the moral line that we dare not cross.

What happens when it does not?

The results are all around us. Benign capitalism becomes ravenous consumerism, where individuals are nothing more than "consumers," ripe for exploitation. Patriotism becomes a loud, unthinking ego-excuse for war. For the privileged few, huge compensations are handed out for behavior that a detached observer would deem immoral, at the expense of the many. Political ambitions make unholy alliances with extremism, which in the end devours the hand that feeds it.

The simple truth is, amoral freedom does not recognize the moral urgings of Telos.

\* \* \*

**When it comes to explaining** the development of life on earth, Darwin's theory of evolution does not recognize such possibilities as divine intervention, forces of destiny, or even the hint of a developmental plan or goal other than an instinct for survival. Our capacity for complex thought is attributed to a mixed bag of genetic mutation and adaptation responding to a competitive environment.

Darwin's theory makes sense, and plenty of evidence has been found to support it. That being said, we should not be swayed by intellectual timidity.

Evolution's mechanized scheme of the world foregoes the idea of destiny or purpose as a romanticized notion based on hindsight or wish fulfillment. It explains the diversity and complexity of life without reference to the miraculous. This preserves the integrity of the scientific method. Mystical, spiritual or religious ideas are considered outside its domain.

It is probably best that way. The complexity of human consciousness does not lend itself well to laboratory analysis. While research certainly produces insights, the results are never satisfying. They lack qualitative aspects that we intuitively need. As a default, we turn to religion and myth to find them.

Early Western philosophers were not so tied to *objective* science that it prevented them from considering *subjective* experience as well. As they speculated about the universe, they still appreciated knowledge gained through their senses and intuition.

In the natural world, they not only *witnessed* birth and growth and transformation, they *contemplated* those changes first hand and depended on them. They concluded that everything that naturally evolves does so from its own nature, its Telos – from birth to childhood to adulthood and beyond. That a caterpillar wraps itself in a cocoon and transforms itself into a moth testifies to this incredible process. This is proof of Telos in action.

Today, the science of genetics *describes* (but cannot explain) how this occurs on the molecular level.

Two thousand years ago, it was concluded that living things have a natural propensity for growth, maturity, and a final end. They postulated what seemed reasonable to their minds and satisfying to their souls. While they gathered facts, postulated hypotheses and sewed them together like any good scientist, they did not limit themselves to that. As philosophers, they asked deeply human questions and tried to answer them.

Lacking Darwin's insight, such notables as Aristotle taught that each separate life had its own developmental goals, its own purpose that progressed from *being* to *becoming*. Their concept of Telos described not only the goals inherent in a thing, but acknowledged the subsequent force, urge or will to fulfill them.

Today's average person straddles a busy world of subjective and objective experiences without trying to appreciate their differences. We accept science. We rely on it. We recognize a dimension to life that defies the scientific method, a dimension that engages the world in a manner that is less predictable but more alive and pertinent to our nature. Simply put, there is more to us than science has yet revealed and we accept that. Our spontaneity and changeableness for example; and our level of consciousness, with its mixed bag of reason, instinct and emotion, always complicates things. We also accept our love for beauty, our respect of virtue for the sake of virtue alone (which often contradicts self-interest), the intricate weavings of love, and the staid mandates of honor. This is the realm of the philosopher, not the scientist.

Because of this, the concept of Telos retains value that scientific materialism has yet to replace.

Telos encompasses the complexities and intuitions of our minds and imbues them with purpose that contributes to our self-development.

* * *

**Telos is part of the** structure and potential of our minds and bodies, within the environment that we live in, that influences who we are and who we become. When recognized, it provides a goal for direction, which is where purpose and meaning is derived.

Telos is related to Areté, the greatest good, because it pushes us toward reason and virtue as part of our unfolding nature.

The theory of human evolution stands out as one of the most influential discoveries of modern times – and one of the most controversial. Like an unfinished story, it ends just at the point where human nature needs to know more. Explaining life materialistically banishes the spiritual elements that humanity has always cherished. These elements have been part of our development for so long that their absence leaves a void that is difficult to fill. With due respect toward atheists and agnostics, most people have need for some sort of spirituality in their lives – however we translate that. Because evolution does not offer this, some people distrust science and secular education. Others turn to New Age philosophies for comfort, which are nothing more than a revival of old age superstitions. Religious cults are on the rise that turn their backs not only on science but on reason as well.

People are not getting what they need from today's intellectual environment. They are not connecting with the nature they are part of in a realistic fashion.

What science lacks, evolution especially, is a *philosophy* based on reason that is inclusive of our experience of the world. We are not robots or computers. Human psychology is always part of the equation. We need an honest philosophy that speaks to that need.

We start by admitting that human evolution is no longer constrained by competitively adaptive survival. The reasoning mind differentiates us from other animals. Our goal is not only to survive, but to *survive well*. Progress among human beings is not limited to passive adaptation. We make progress happen. We make choices and formulate plans.

Telos recognizes that. It provides the human sciences with a foundation for a progressive philosophy that includes Areté and Aletheia, and much more. Its spiritual nature is not derived from some other world, but is part of our own direct experience – no frills attached.

This is vitally important.

The culture that believes in reason and personal industry reaps the reward of technological advancement. Likewise, the community that embraces virtue enjoys the benefits of authentic living, which includes love, honor, respect, and cooperation. Freedom is part of that dynamic.

Telos includes all these attributes. It inspires us away from mediocrity in order to live heroically. When ignored, the loss of personal meaning and purpose leaves us incomplete, frustrated and unfulfilled. This frustration comes from knowing, deep inside, that our lives are meant to be significant, not wasted on ego or entertainment or consumerism.

\* \* \*

**When we respond to** our *inner aim,* we influence the formation of our destiny by becoming a more active, determining part of our own evolution.

Admittedly, the actual fulfillment of that aim may be questionable or at best imperfect. Nevertheless, it is important to understand that the thinking, deciding mind constantly makes choices that shapes its direction and final result. Life not only makes it possible for us to consciously attain our own completeness, it prompts us to lead lives that are dedicated to that goal.

Today's knight-errant is someone who takes such personal commitments seriously. His direction is clear, despite all the uncertainty that life brings with it, because he subjects his self-will to the dictates of conscience and the learning process of the quest.

Telos moves us toward the very best of what human nature predisposes, which is the combination of reason and virtuous compassion of Areté.

Consider the completeness of such a person. Reasoning is sharp. Values strong and clear. Honesty certain. Conscience activated. Compassion alive. Inner aim focused. Each discovery furthers the understanding of truth in the relational format of Aletheia. Areté is constantly engaged. Advocating for virtue branches out to everyone.

Telos insists that such nobility is our birthright and obligation.

Unfortunately, this birthright does not just happen on its own.

We must strive for it through the quality of our lives, which brings our *deeper quest* into focus.

\* \* \*

**We experience Telos** as a wordless, inner aim, related to conscience, that provokes fulfillment when embraced, and discontent when ignored.

The quest provides a meaningful experience of life from which we learn and grow and discover our power to make a difference. This self-development nurtures reason and virtue, which are the mainstays of Areté. As our experience continues, everything becomes clearer. Confidence grows. Some of us are fortunate enough to experience *anagnorisis,* a transformative awakening that solidifies our progress. We become what we were meant to be according to our potential.

Eyes wide open, the knight-errant encounters truth as Aletheia, and is ready to face the world.

\* \* \*

*What does this mean for us?*
Telos can be likened to an inner voice or guide that tries to influence the *general* direction of our lives and that of our species as a whole. *Specific* direction is a matter of conscious decision. Our paths are not set in stone. They are contingent upon variables of the moment, such as jobs, family life, career choices, social obligations, etc. We cannot avoid being influenced by what surrounds us in our everyday lives.

We are also limited by our inability to see the greater picture of things, including how we fit in. Telos reminds us that every moment of consciousness is a point in an unpredictable continuum. Far from insignificant, each moment decides every-thing that follows. That infuses our experience in time with incredible responsibility. Since every choice influences the world around us, our decisions are far more significant than they seem. This makes the attainment of personal nobility not only possible but important. Telos encourages us to participate in a scale of truth much grander than most of us realize.

Knowing this is not always comforting. Life is not a game we play, winner takes all. Political strategies that hold no regard for truth and compassion, that care little about the values that they claim to extol, that refuse to consider the consequences of short-term agendas, that prefer crippling, nonsensical contention to serious dialog, work against the greater Telos of humanity. Responsibility for the future is discarded, along with any semblance of truth, justice and hope.

If we cannot take pride in the direction that we are heading as people, as communities, and as a species, then we are failing our own Telos. We are regressing. Thanks to the capabilities of technology and globalization, the times are such that we cannot afford such regression – not even for a moment. The problems we face are too formidable.

## Chapter 7

# Ordo Mundi—*Order of the World*

**At first glance, it would seem** that today's world has little need for a modern version of knights in shining armor. The first firearms ended that profession long ago. We live in a world of cluster-bombs, pop-psychology, and cynicism.

That being said, the world that we live in has great need for men and women of strong integrity and high ideals, everyday people who are committed to living their lives rightly. In fact, the need has never been greater.

The aim of Chivalry-Now is to help us to become such people.

Simply put, the world we live in is our domain. It is our place and home from cradle to grave. We are instinctively called upon to care about those around us and protect them from harm. In the Grail legends, the king not only represented the well-being of his people, but the good of his realm as a whole. This included the land and natural resources. When the Grail King was wounded, his suffering brought ruin to everything. This is a lesson for all who strive for the mantle of leadership. A once thriving sanctuary where the holiest of relics continued to reside became a *Wasteland*. This reminds us that even those whose qualities serve as a blessing to the world are still capable of doing much harm.

It does well to remember that the Grail King was wounded in his manhood, a prescient warning for males today. When our ethics become unbalanced or go astray, the world pays a heavy price.

It is plain to see that the world of nature is being harmed by pollution of our making, abusive exploitation and widespread indifference. We see that global climates are changing. According to scientists who monitor such things, the speed of those changes is surpassing previous predictions. Species are being threatened. Resources are being depleted without concern for the needs of future generations. Air and water purity are so tainted that incidents of cancer and asthma are constantly on the rise.

Despite all the warnings, increased health problems, and stark evidence of climate change, many of us close our eyes as if the world had no value in itself – as if it were somehow indebted *to us* for our pleasure, ready to be sacrifice upon the altar of greed. Instead of taking strong, heroic action to protect our world, we relinquish power to sociopathic leaders who purposely knock heads in political gridlock.

The times call for conscientious action. The cost of delay and obstinacy has been steep already. The world that we depend upon needs to be rescued. Rescuing the defenseless is what knighthood is all about.

We know that innocent lives are at stake, along with those of future generations. Greed and complacency always find ways to distort the obvious and confuse the well-meaning. When political ideologies defy the needs of our planet, consider the gauntlet thrown at our feet.

Rescuing the environment is no simple task. It will take sacrifice and commitment from us all. The longer we wait, the greater the cost and difficulties. The legend of the Holy Grail, with its references to the Wasteland and the wound of male pride, was child's play in comparison. One heroic Sir Percival is no longer enough. We must all become heroes of conscience.

To sit back and watch our world deteriorate – or worse, to greedily contribute to its demise – is the epitome of dishonor and the cause for deepest shame. The earth is our domain. What are we if we do not safeguard it with every ounce of our being? What kind of men and women would we be if we refuse to take responsibility for our actions? Are we so blinded by ego gratification that we have lost our entire perspective? Is our concept of freedom so infantile that we cannot step forward as men and women of conscience and do what is right?

What happened to the ideals that our Western civilization was founded on? What happened to reason? Has our sense of honor been totally negated by frivolous pride?

A burning house is not saved by pretending that there is no fire. Dousing it with gasoline, just because we can, only makes the problem worse. As every firefighter knows, the challenge demands an immediate reservoir of bravery, resources and commitment.

*Today's chivalry is meaningless if it is not relevant for the times we live in – if it does not respond to the actual threats that face us.* The intent of Chivalry-Now is to inspire a vanguard of committed men and women who will heal not only the ills of society, but the world of nature as well.

* * *

**Esoterica takes** our relationship to nature into account.

During the Middle Ages, when chivalry was at its height, Christian theologians pondered a concept that they called *Ordo Mundi,* which is Latin for the *Order of the World.*

Ordo Mundi refers to the dynamic inter-relatedness of all things. In this respect, it is somewhat comparable to the Eastern concept of *Tao.* In medieval times, of course, it differed significantly from its Eastern counterpart due to theological influence. It recognized the workings of God's plan within Creation, rather than nature representing ultimate truth itself. Enlightenment thinkers later referred to these workings as divine *Providence.* Today, we simply call it *nature.*

Ordo Mundi recognizes the symbiotic interrelationship of all things and the natural laws that govern them. It concludes that things exist the way they do according to God's plan, which deserves to be honored and respected and, whenever possible, learned from. The Christian perspective points out that the God of Genesis declared his creation *good*, and it should be treated as such. At the same time, the influence of Stoic philosophy called for our relationship with nature to be based on spiritual reverence.

The medieval mind had no understanding of nature as science has explained it in the last three centuries. Nevertheless, they understood quite well that their lives were completely dependent upon it, as our lives continue to depend on it now. They purposely and intuitively held their fingers to the pulse of nature's deeper meaning, of which they were invariably a part. They relied on its benevolence. They sought to articulate its poetry. They were cognizant of its mystery. Nature fashioned all of their experiences.

This symbiotic relationship differed sharply from our antiseptic homes with temperature control, indoor jobs, super-market harvests, and reliance on money for survival. Despite the inherent difficulties of a pre-scientific world, the immediate relationship with nature made people constantly aware of their place in the universe. It was a daily, subjective experience.

In today's world, we tend to separate *objectivity* from *subjectivity,* as if these two perspectives of reality had no relationship at all, yet each holds a proper purpose that should be respected.

Objectivity is vitally important to the scientific method and to our own social evolution. This is so obvious that it needs no explanation. But that does not mean that subjectivity should be deprecated from our psychological makeup. Our every thought, even our presence as an objective observer, is intrinsically subjective. We cannot escape it.

Areté, which includes reason and compassion, represents an idealized combination of these two approaches to knowledge – virtuous, inquisitive, critical in judgment, yet humbly fallible, striving for improvement. This combination is our most significantly human trait, which discovers itself most fully through the quest.

On the other hand, contrary to reason and inhibitive to Areté, is the false perception that we are somehow separate from nature – living in a world of which we are not really a part. Many of us fall into that trap despite all evidence to the contrary. Why? Because it allows us to turn away from a healthy relationship with nature in order to exploit it beyond our needs. Our principles have been diverted by the ravenous demands of greed. In many ways we have become greed's progeny. We have been taught in many and subtle ways to believe its destructive lie.

We watch untouched from the safety of our televisions as hurricanes and floods decimate whole communities. We zoom around in cars without regard for the dangerous speeds that we travel. We equate celebrity with *stardom* as if actors were somehow favored by the gods and worthy of adulation. We resist aging with creams, cosmetics and surgeries. The result? We anesthetize ourselves from the realities of nature, while hurricanes, traffic fatalities and old-age continually ignore all our efforts.

By perceiving ourselves as separate from nature, we adopt a mindset that embraces illusion rather than truth. Taken to the extreme, illusion becomes our drug of choice, even when it distracts us from the obligations that predicate our very existence. Why else would we unashamedly treat the earth, our only home and the birthplace of humanity, as a garbage heap?

The ideals and values of Chivalry-Now help us see through that. When we tap into our moral centers, think for ourselves, question things, and engage in life as a quest, we are more apt to gauge everything we encounter according to its truer value. When we encounter nature as a catalyst for learning, the reverence that follows helps complete who we are.

Today's knight who seeks the solace of contemplation does not venture off to the big city or shopping mall to find it. Like the Grail-Knights of legend, we go out into the forest, listen to babbling brooks, sit patiently on a hill or cliff while appreciating the brilliant colors of the setting sun. We hear the call of Mystery in bird songs and the whirring of crickets. The stars intimate eternity. Fresh, clean air reminds us of nature's beneficence. Like Jesus and Mohammed and so many others, we move away from the crowds in order to claim our spiritual benediction.

In simple terms, Ordo Mundi can be viewed as a direct study and appreciation of nature through a merger of intellect and intuition. It involves the whole person in a relationship of I/Thou, rather than I/It. More correctly, it is a relationship of child/parent, where nature serves as the parent. In this way we discover not just facts, which certainly have value of their own, but our place in the universe. We knowingly participate in the here and now.

A stroll in the forest, a moment's reflection by a running stream, a sunset of dramatic colors spread across the sky, the creeping stillness of twilight, still provide us with timeless connections to our own inner consciousness like nothing else can. Here we find the embrace of comfort and security that transcends the distractions of everyday life. Here we find a special affirmation that words cannot convey. Nature has provided this for countless millennia – an inspiration for mystics, poets and scientists alike.

When the distractions of technology interfere with this transmission, it damages the intricate balance of who we are. The completeness of human nature demands that we maintain this connection.

The quest affirms this.

\* \* \*

**When we do something wrong,** facing the responsibility that follows is no easy task. It requires strength, integrity and character to admit our guilt, repent of our misdeeds and set about to correct the situation.

When we do the wrong thing over and over again, and fashion our lifestyles to depend upon it, facing guilt becomes almost impossible. We find excuses to keep things the way they are, no matter what the consequences. As with alcohol or drug addiction, we simply ignore right and wrong and the needs of others. The more we do so, the easier it becomes. Part of our conscience shuts down, which impacts other areas of our lives.

When we refuse to fight the good fight, we turn our backs on the soul of chivalry. We become part of the problem. We may do this out of pride, deficits in character, fear of change, the desire to contradict those who disagree with us or, as many of our leaders do, out of the lust for wrongful profits.

We should ask ourselves how many slices of conscience can be discarded before nothing is left?

While the failure of conscience applies to many problems, it is strongly evident in our relationship to the environment and non-human life. Pollution, exploitation, a complete disregard for what is environmentally sound, has shifted the natural balance of things. We go on with our lives as if the sword of Damocles were not hanging by a thread, ready to fall. We obsess over political one-upmanship and celebrity vices as if these distractions somehow relieve us of our culpabilities. Meaningless thoughts subvert our attention and distract us from what needs to be done.

To claim ignorance now is to admit that we willingly and knowingly choose to be ignorant. We were sufficiently warned by the scientific community decades earlier. The warnings were repeated as signs of climate change became more apparent. Once it became a political issue, instead of employing mature deliberation on what to do, we subject the safety of our planet to the hands of power plays and obstructionism. That such a gargantuan threat is being relegated to the theatrical gamesmanship of political rhetoric shows how capable we are of moving away from reason and conscience – and toward death.

Sometimes I fear that it is already too late. We find ourselves clinging to the edge of an abyss of our own making, ready to fall, our grip loosening.

I am no scientist – but then, I have no need to be. I live in the world where the indicators of climate change have advanced unabated for years. We see it all around us, with tragic consequences in some parts of the world. I hear dire warnings from respected scientists, and they seem reasonable – enough to make necessary changes.

Others say that the climate is changing, but not as a result of human activity. Their reasoning suggests we can pump incredible amounts of carbon and other pollutants into our finite atmosphere without dangerous consequences. That simply defies common sense. These special interests hire professional consultants to back up their dangerous claims. They have no proof, of course. Their mission is to sow doubt, allowing the problems to continue.

The past extinction of thousands of species proves that the workings and balance of nature are complex, interconnected and surprisingly fragile. It makes no allowance for ignorance or ideology. It is terrifying to think that a chain of events in the biosphere may have already started that cannot be reversed.

How should we respond?

Certainly not by insulting the miracle of life with political gamesmanship.

While our brightest minds make it clear that they do not know all there is about global warming, those of less caliber are willing to risk everything by denying evidence that is plain to see. Our only moral recourse is to pull ourselves away from this abyss and hope we are not too late.

We start by recognizing how greed, commercialism and political ideologies have worked together to distort our values toward nature. If we do not view the world with reverence, as something to love, care for and defend like family, then we are the enemies of every living creature on earth – including ourselves.

We belong to this planet. It does not belong to us. If we continue to shirk our responsibilities, we deserve whatever tragedy awaits us. But what of those innocents of the world, children and impoverished people, that we condemn as well? Have we no responsibility toward them?

Our ideals tell us to support just causes. What cause could possibly be more important?

For Chivalry-Now, saving the world for posterity is not just the latest cause célèbre. It is a call to motivate all persons of conscience to immediate action.

* * *

**Contemplating Ordo Mundi** provides us with a portion of our humanity that we would otherwise lack.

Nature constantly confronts the human intellect with the wonder of Creation itself, with the transience of time, with an appreciation of the interconnectedness and symbiosis of all living things. It provides us with what legal scholars and philosophers alike refer to as *Nature's Law*, an important topic that we will also cover. This is all part of our maturation toward completeness.

Ordo Mundi helps us turn away from self-indulgence. It allows us to return as prodigal sons and daughters who understand our indebtedness to nature.

It is not my intent to overly romanticize nature, or adorn it with mystical implications that are misleading. Nature can be harsh and unfeelingly cruel. It not only gives life, it takes it away. In fact, all kinds of suffering that we seek to avoid are part of nature in one way or another.

Nevertheless, nature is both vital and inseparable to our existence. It is destructively wrong to believe that we are less dependent on nature than our ancestors were. Everything we are part of depends on nature, every minute of the day.

Many of our romanticized notions, however, are not based on fantasy. They are based on direct experience and carry significance that we can learn from. When we free our conscious minds from jaded cynicism, it is possible to sense whispers of affirmation in the sound of a waterfall or running brook. When we are fortunate enough to hear them, tree frogs lull us to sleep with persistent reassurance. Chirping birds enliven our hearts. A beautiful sky launches our consciousness toward heaven, while the moon humbles us with hints of eternal transience. When instincts merge with intellect, our awareness of nature is able to transcend our mundane, mind-numbing routines in ways that we can scarcely comprehend. The rewards are clear. We respond to nature in ways that are natural to who we are.

Anthropologists tell us that nature provided the first classroom and curriculum for our species. It not only shaped us, it still offers hints of possibilities. The recognition of a single world and a common humanity has the power to unite us all. Believers and nonbelievers alike recognize aspects of nature that they hold sacred. Contemplations of existence might be instigated by the catalyst of a rock.

As children of the twenty-first century, constantly subjected to life-suppressing cynicism, undeserved hubris, and a daily arrogance toward nature that borders on blasphemous, we need to ask ourselves: how can we regain a positive, life-affirming relationship?

Are we more curse than blessing to the very planet upon which we depend?

The answer is found in our everyday choices.

If we approach these choices humbly, we find that the ideals of Chivalry-Now tap into an undercurrent of innocence that still exists despite a lifetime of commercial brainwashing. Here we find our pristine selves waiting to be reborn.

It is part of our Areté to discover and articulate meaning that would otherwise never be articulated. That, in itself, tells us to protect rather than destroy, uphold truth rather than give substance to lies, and bring honor into the world, along with forgiveness, generosity and fair play.

Surely that is human nature at its best.

\* \* \*

**I have often witnessed patches** of early morning fog lift quietly from the pond behind my house. Wispy tendrils drift so slowly that they appear to be still. In such moments time itself seems to stop, inviting a pause favorable to wandering thoughts and impressions.

These occasions produce an innocence that only nature can provide and the human mind recognize. For me, I imagine hints of Camelot or Avalon lingering in the phantom mist – not swordplay or stone piled castles, but a wordless poetry of spiritual romance – a feeling born in nature that, despite everything, insists that all is right in the world. I see in that lazy mist a new and better world waiting to be born.

Such experiences are regarded as fantasy. What is real, however, is what stirs inside us when they happen. We are reminded that dreams not only have their own reality, they have their own purpose as well. Just like thought and memory, imagination exists in the realm of the mind.

As any writer or artist will tell you, dreams are brought to life by *inspiration*. Nature is a fine source by which to be inspired.

The purpose of poetry, myth and dreams is to express elements of the subconscious that cannot otherwise be expressed. Its language is made up of symbols preserved in culture through ritual and tradition. We create them spontaneously. The mechanisms of thought that we so identify with come from this dynamic.

When we speak of Ordo Mundi, the order of the world, we are

speaking of a realm from which we are inseparable. We should honor it appropriately. If we do not, something of our ideals remains incomplete.

The essence of Oro Mundi is universal. We find glimpses of it wherever people exist. Pagan and animistic religions are derived from this reverential intimacy with nature. Pantheism enjoys its perennial resurgence from similar views. In the bible, we encounter the *Shekinah* (the feminine aspect of *Yahweh*, also known as *Sophia*, or *Wisdom*,). Mystics of Islam recognize its presence.

For those of us who engage life as a quest, Ordo Mundi urges us to look upon nature as a fount of spirituality – not for worship, but as a concrete expression of Mystery. The only solid proof we have.

We understand the world very differently than our ancestors did. A high-school science text would debunk almost everything believed about nature during the Middle Ages. What these science books are incapable of doing however, is establishing a living, breathing, vital relationship with nature. They do not open our hearts to the spiritual significance that our ancestors enjoyed for millennia sitting around a fire or gathering herbs.

Science has made it possible to understand the universe like never before, even at the molecular level. Nevertheless, if we are intellectually honest, we must humbly recognize that the Mystery of existence remains untouched.

What Mystery points to, however, is real – as real as the mind that senses it. Ordo Mundi teaches us how to approach that Mystery through existence itself.

As long as seasons change, storms threaten, mountains shake, people die, and the arrival of spring still elicits joy, our obligation toward nature's Mystery, which is inextricably connected to life itself, is *reverence*.

To adequately appreciate this experience, it would help to shut-off our cell phones now and then, tear ourselves away from televisions and computer screens, and put aside intoxicants, including those of anger and competition. Only then can we reacquaint ourselves with the spellbinding silence through which Mystery still whispers to our hearts.

\* \* \*

**Historically, our reverence** for nature predates our reverence for traditions. Indeed, traditions often represented, celebrated or sought to facilitate the ways of nature. Consider rites-of-passage, harvest festivals, solstice celebrations and the welcoming of life that each springtime generates. Trees were held sacred by the Celts. Lightning was considered the weapon of Zeus. Ritual sacrifices were made to assure that winter would pass and the planting season take its place. The changing of the seasons, and the life-cycles of plants spawned from buried seed, hinted at reincarnation and immortality. Hunting societies honored the symbiotic relationship between predators and prey that dictated their means of survival.

Nature has always taken part in the process of humanizing people and societies. Unfortunately this is changing as the wonders of technology take up more and more of our attention. For many of us, cell phones dominate even a walk in the park. MP3 players replace the sounds of nature that were once an everyday part of the human experience.

This is a major deviation from our past. We have no idea what it means, or where it will lead. One might suspect an eventual disconnection from reality as computer entertainments become more real. Even now we are witnessing priorities shift beneath our feet, and scarcely consider their implications. This should concern us all. It takes only one generation for much to be lost, and we have been losing our cultural inheritance since the Industrial Age, when progress was measured by the number of smoke stacks that polluted major cities.

The biggest problem we face, and the least recognized, is that *we are living a lie,* a grand illusion that pulls us away from nature's reality. No matter how much we try, or convince ourselves otherwise, we cannot remove ourselves from nature. We depend on it for everything. While human progress has always included a blind ignorance to its results, never has it been so integrated in all that we do.

The truth is, we are physically part of nature's ecosystem. Good hygiene alone keeps the barnyard odors of our bodies at bay. Our waste does not miraculously disappear once the trash is picked up. It merely gathers somewhere else. Gravity prevents us from flying off into space. Air brings life-sustaining oxygen to our lungs. Sunlight nourishes not only our souls, but the plants and animals that we feed on. We cannot live long without water.

For our own sake, and for the sake of justice, we must look to understanding the world we live in with a sincere respect and regard for life. *All life.* It is a crime against the universe to sacrifice the health of our planet and the survival of future generations just to satisfy the greed of one generation.

Judging by toxic waste sites, the poisoning of our oceans and waterways, and the tepid response to global warming, we are shirking our gravest responsibilities.

\* \* \*

**Metaphorically speaking,** like the Grail Knights of legend, today's knight errant purposely engages the quest by entering the forest of life where the woods are thickest. There are no trodden paths to follow. It is a starting point that is undistracted by the noise of the marketplace or demands of others. Here we are challenged to find the sacred – not as fantasy would have it, but as the Mystery that it really is. Just as the Grail was thought to be a physical cup made holy by the Mystery surrounding it, we can find distinctive wonder in everything we see when our heart allows it. This includes our own existence as well. With eyes to see and ears to hear, one need only to look and listen to know that Mystery abounds everywhere. Placing society's ego-centric lure behind us, we confront the world of nature just like the Grail Knights before us – to test and cleanse our souls.

It is no coincidence that we usually experience our most personal initiation, our *anagnorisis*, alone in the presence of nature's beauty. Spiritual maturation is common in such encounters. We are less for the lack of them. Break that connection, believe the lie that we are separate from the world that nourishes us at every moment, and we surrender our integrity to illusion. We need to reestablish that connection in order to move forward.

Nature remains important to our lives, both psychologically and spiritually. Jesus went into the desert for 40 days before starting his mission, and always removed himself from others to pray in private. Mohammed retreated to a cave for his spiritual encounter. Buddha found enlightenment under the Bodhi tree, away from the clamor of the city. King Arthur retrieved Excalibur from the middle of a lake. The Grail Knights were spiritually tested while wandering the forests in search of the Holy Grail.

Legend has it that when the Grail King was wounded in the genitals, his entire kingdom suffered devastation in response. Rich forests and fertile valleys degenerated into a Wasteland. Farms fell to ruin and everyone was deprived of life's pleasures.

The lesson to be learned is simple. When the nobility of human energy is diverted by pride and disconnected from its source, the whole world suffers. This is especially true today. It took the innocent compassion of Sir Perceval to repair that, a knight raised in nature's woods, whom others considered a fool.

\* \* \*

**In the face of our present condition,** when human arrogance threatens the course and survival of nature itself, we need to ask ourselves what lies at the root of so much apathy.

For over a century we have measured success by how much waste we generate, the useless toys we pile in the garage, and the amount of debt that we accumulate.

When we hear dire warnings about environmental pollution, we either deny or ignore them, or just arrogantly continue as we were. Like Pavlov's dogs, we have been systematically trained by reward and punishment to let greed override conscience.

Climate change did not happen for lack of knowledge or adequate warning. Scientists clearly told us what to expect over 40 years ago, with warnings repeated every step of the way.

A fellow I knew some years ago was very honest about it. With a certain amount of pride he said: "Why should we care about global warming? We won't be around when it happens."

Such words convey a poverty of conscience that comes from a lifetime of cultivating selfishness. And while most people might intellectually disagree with him, their lives reflect the same attitude – more of a dodge than a conviction. The difference between a lack of conscience and shutting off one's conscience is negligible.

It is true that the worst consequences of today's pollution will be borne by generations to come, even though the results are arriving quicker than expected. Most of us will be dead when the worst arrives. If we continue on the way we are now, we will be cursed by those who follow us as the world's worst generation, and deservedly so.

At the same time, we are also losing the best part of what it means to be human. By sacrificing our souls to willful ignorance, we betray not only humanity but all of life, and the billions of years that evolution invested to create it.

The resurgence of a warrior's ethic is needed to turn all this around. I fear that nothing less will suffice.

## Chapter 8

# Reason—*The Glory of Humankind*

"To a reasoning being, an act that accords with nature is an act that accords with reason." (Marcus Aurelius, Book 7, line 11)

"It is the mind, or reason, which is the predominant element in us who are human creatures; it is this which renders a human being human and distinguishes him essentially and generically from the brute." (Pope Leo XIII)

"He that takes away reason to make way for revelation puts out the light of both..." (John Locke)

**The ancient Greeks,** along with Stoics like Marcus Aurelius and many other great thinkers in the West, believed that the ability to reason was the glory of human nature, a prominent aspect of Areté that was meant to go hand-in-hand with virtue. It was in the soil of these ancient ponderings where democracy first gained its foothold as a form of government. Alongside democracy came schools of philosophy and mathematics where the foundations of scientific theory were devised. Art reached new pinnacles of realism and perfection. Architecture fashioned designs of beauty that still inspire us. Outdoor theaters, acoustically designed, presented dramas, tragedies and comedies that shaped the course of Western thought and literature to this day.

All this happened in less than two centuries that were repeatedly interrupted by war.

Outdoor academies offered no desks, much less laptops and calculators. Tools were primitive at best. The knowledge base that they inherited was racked with superstition.

Skill, imagination, intellectual integrity and *a strong belief in human potential* compensated for all these handicaps. These thinkers not only questioned the world around them, they questioned their own answers. They concluded that only repeated testing could produce the kind of certainty that progress could depend on.

They also believed in confronting ignorance and limitations, resulting in a strong belief that they could shape their own destiny.

And so they did. Their achievements shone like beacons throughout the intellectual darkness, and inspire us still when we let them.

Mediterranean cultures adopted and perpetuated Greek accomplishments. They became *Hellenized*. Rome did especially, where copies of Greek art and architecture dominated major cities, libraries preserved knowledge, and a republican form of government made its début.

When Rome eventually fell in the fifth century, after a long decline, the result was an intellectual regression into Dark Age tribalism. The Church preserved what teachings it could, while feudalism maintained a repressive regime controlled by warlords and chieftains.

Out of this intellectual hibernation, chivalry was born as a warrior ethic, reinstating a higher sense of justice, moral obligation, and courtesy. In southern France, individualism was further encouraged by a new addition, *romantic love*.

Through chivalry, a resurgence of Western ideals once again flourished in song and literature, incorporating archetypal images and mythical themes. During the High Middle Ages, it was obvious that something refined and definitive had reasserted itself into Western culture.

This was assisted by the crusades. As warriors became acquainted with the advanced culture of the Muslim world, they rediscovered the teachings of ancient Greece and Rome that were not only preserved but richly expounded. Taking back this wealth of knowledge, Europe reclaimed its own intellectual legacy, which spread like wildfire. The Western mind had been reborn.

As reason gained its foothold, progress quickly followed. Philosophy added a richness of meaning that sharply criticized superstition and intolerance. Hovels, chapels and ale halls were replaced by houses, cathedrals and palaces. Skilled artisans and thinkers gained the respect and compensation that they deserved. Michelangelo, da Vinci, Galileo, Columbus, Dante, Mirandola, Erasmus, Luther – all geniuses in their own respects, steered the direction of Western culture toward a progressive future. Merchants flourished as capitalism destroyed the bonds of feudalism.

This spark of reason ignited a powder keg of human potential and creativity. Church intellectuals systematically embraced reason, and often led the way in promoting free inquiry, despite some unfortunate lapses. It was soon decided that science and religion could respect and even compliment each other from their own separate realms of expertise.

We aptly refer to this period as the *Renaissance*, which is French for *rebirth*.

In the wake of the Renaissance, the 17$^{th}$ and 18$^{th}$ centuries became flooded by another wave of intellectuals who extolled the benefits of reason. The revolutionary ideas of Bacon and Newton were quickly followed by those of Locke and Voltaire, and a number of other great thinkers. This culminated in what we now refer to as the *Age of Reason*, or *Age of Enlightenment*.

Encouraging free thought, these inspired geniuses sparked a new optimism based on human potential. They applied reason to everything and were rewarded with one success after the other. With each new scientific discovery, they were convinced that the secrets of the universe were not only approachable but understandable as well. This included social and governmental ideas as well. The wording of the *Declaration of Independence* of the United States, and the Constitution that followed, stand as testaments to Enlightenment philosophy.

From today's vantage point of advanced technology, we find much of their optimism justified. Many of nature's secrets have been profitably uncovered along with new discoveries every day. While scientists respectfully concede that there are limits to human understanding, the popular imagination, nourished by microchips and the magic of the entertainment industry, challenge those limits every day.

The possibilities that reason offers appear to be endless, and should not be limited to the purview of philosophers and scientists. The capacity for reason defines who we are as human beings. Everyone of sound mind holds a germ of genius in some capacity. It needs only to be found and exercised. When we fail in that regard, we fall short of our true potential. Personal authenticity fails to assert itself. What meaning the universe offers escapes us.

\* \* \*

**Reason plays an important part** in every aspect of our lives. *Chivalry-Now* readily asserts that intelligence and rational thinking vitally contribute to our quest experience.

Reason prompts us to make better decisions in our lives, and avoid falling prey to exploitation. It helps us become more competent in all aspects of our lives.

Reason fosters responsibility, which gives freedom its intrinsic value and makes personal autonomy a reachable goal. Using knowledgeable discernment for self-development is what *positive freedom* is all about. Anything less is a formula for ruin.

Irrational people are often considered not responsible for their actions. Since the human concept of freedom is inseparable from responsibility, we conclude that people who cannot or will not act reasonably are not technically free. How can they be, when they are controlled by the irrational forces of life, easily led astray by others, intimidated by peer pressure, enslaved by desires, or so plagued by constant errors that autonomy becomes a farce?

The freedom that such people want, and will even fight to attain, is limited to *negative or lazy freedom*, which is merely the absence of outside restraints.

Some believe that positive and negative freedom have nothing to do with one another.

They are wrong. Both are necessary for human nature to fulfill itself.

*Positive freedom* more capably thrives in an environment of few restraints, in which personal responsibility is basic. Without the potential given by negative freedom, it must struggle to exist.

*Negative freedom* by itself, lacking the positive direction of growth and purpose, and the activation of conscience, presents a recipe for stagnation and a host of social problems – many of which we suffer from today.

What makes the difference is that positive freedom encourages the use of enlightened reason as part of the human paradigm that makes us complete.

Depending on how we use it, reason and virtue define who we are as persons. Ancient Greeks understood that in their concept of Areté, which is the excellent functioning of the virtuous, rational mind.

Reason gives us the capacity for making us capable, confident and reliable. It can also foster idealism in realistic terms, shaping the age we live in as sensible, progressive and cooperative.

Facing all the major problems that plague us today, the use of clear reason, dedicated to the good, will determine not only our personal survival but the continuation of our species.

Misguided or underutilized, it opens the door to eventual destruction.

\* \* \*

The *Age of Enlightenment* offers a profound inspiration to Chivalry-Now. While medieval chivalry provides it with a foundation and pedigree, and the insight to confront life as a quest, the Enlightenment introduces a wide spectrum of insights that strongly influences the uniqueness of the Western mind. There are great benefits to becoming familiar with this fascinating movement that transformed all of Europe and the Americas – and eventually left its mark on the rest of the world as well.

The Enlightenment flourished during the 17$^{th}$ and 18$^{th}$ centuries, representing a natural progression of free thought that originated in classical Greece. It re-established our cultural/ philosophical direction with a jubilant burst of intellectual curiosity.

Before it, formal education was limited to the study of Aristotle and Homer, as if true wisdom could not be gleaned from anywhere else. Originality was restrained to interpreting the wisdom of antiquity, which severely limited intellectual progress.

Dark Age superstition remained fixed in a world that people little understood. The failure of a crop might lead to charges of witchcraft, in which innocent people, so accused, were then tortured and killed. Regional conflicts and religious wars decimated entire populations. Disease was treated by counter-effective remedies, such as bloodletting and noxious fumes. The benefits of hygiene were unknown. Western civilization was locked in a state of privileges for the few, and thankless, back-breaking work for everyone else – all determined by birth. Beneath this feudal stasis, however, the dormant potential of the Western mind lay waiting to be reborn.

And then it happened. A catalyst in the 16$^{th}$ century sparked an explosion of intellectual curiosity that could no longer be restrained.

*Francis Bacon* (1561-1626), the English statesman and philosopher, bravely stood up to the intellectual status quo by challenging the limits imposed by classical education and theological interference. He espoused a new method for finding truth, one that involved thoughtful hypothesis and experimentation. He encouraged people to question long held beliefs that were previously regarded as sacrosanct.

Almost single-handedly, Francis Bacon broke the chains of Dark Age inhibitions. He believed that scientific knowledge, then known as the *philosophy of Nature*, provided the means to alleviate human suffering and enhance the quality and happiness of people's lives.

In spiritual matters he separated scientific inquiry from religious interpretation so that both could thrive unimpeded. By redefining the relationship between religion and secular government, he rescued future generations from the religious wars from which Europe previously suffered.

Bacon merely opened the door to what followed. The list of Enlightenment notables is quite impressive:

*John Locke* (1632-1704) explored how the human mind works. He convincingly argued that all knowledge arises from experience. We are born with minds that he described as *"tabula rasa,"* a blank slate, upon which we record what we learn as memory that we then use for future reference. The accumulation and integration of these memories turns into knowledge. While he concluded that we are all products of our environments, he was convinced that we could surpass our limitations through reason, experimentation and confirmation. We can deduce propositions that can then be tested for their validity. He demonstrated that even the complexities of nature can be analyzed by studying their parts and how they interrelate.

We take these truths for granted nowadays. At the time of their inception these revolutionary ideas shook the Western world. People were starting to liberate the way they thought.

Understanding how the mind works is no small thing. It influences everything that follows – in science, psychology, relationships and future directions. It allows us to choose what values we believe according to reason and efficacy. It is difficult to comprehend the impact of John Locke's writing. Together with Francis Bacon, he introduced the Enlightenment movement, which made the birth of the modern mind possible. *Thomas Jefferson*, an ardent supporter of Enlightenment thinking, considered Locke one of the greatest people who ever lived. He borrowed heavily from him when writing the *Declaration of Independence*.

In France, *Rene Descartes* (1596-1650), in his quest for clarity and order, insisted that the mechanics of the natural world could only be understood through a proper, empirical approach toward learning. After centuries of knowledge being restricted to the interpretations of Aristotle and Canon Law, Descartes insisted that real knowledge could only come through direct and systematic inquiry that begins from a position of doubt.

Mathematician and scientist *Galileo Galilei* (1564-1642) challenged the status quo by defending the heliocentric observations of *Copernicus*. When he was duly punished by the Church for doing so, the incident eventually tore down religious barriers to science.

*Isaac Newton* (1643-1727) focused his genius on proving that nature could be mathematically analyzed to formulate *scientific laws*. His own accomplishments well illustrated the potential of the human mind. During an 18 month hiatus from school due to plague, he developed the foundations of calculus and formulated the theories of gravitation, motion, planetary motion and light. He did all that in his early 20s.

*Julien Offroy de La Mettrie* (1709-1751) set about to prove that the efficacy of medical treatments could be improved through empirical research, thus replacing techniques based on superstition. He introduced the development of modern medicine that we benefit from today.

At the age of 26, the inspired *Cesare Beccaria* (1738-1794) drew upon the energy of Enlightenment principles to publish his famous work *On Crime and Punishments*. In it, he pleaded on "behalf of reason and humanity." The incredible popularity of this book helped launch the humanitarian outlook of his age, which led to the development of a liberal conscience in Europe, a conscience based on reason.

*Denis Diderot* (1713-1784) edited and published the extensive *Encyclopedie*, a collection of the writings of the very best minds of the age on a wide variety of subjects, thus preserving the genius of the Enlightenment for future generations.

*Johannes Kepler* (1571-1630) discovered three laws of planetary motion.

The philosophy of *Thomas Hobbes* (1588-1679) encompassed a system that included physics, human nature, politics, and materialism.

*Blaise Pascal* (1623-1662) won acclaim for his amazing accomplishments in the mechanics of calculations, hydrodynamics, geometry, and barometrics.

*Charles-Louis de Secondat*, better known as *Baron de Montesqieu* (1689-1755), became a highly influential political theorist. His work on the fall of the Roman Republic laid the political groundwork for discussion among the founders of the United States, helping them construct a government comprised of separate but equal branches of power.

The above-mentioned names only scratch the surface of Enlightenment writers and philosophers, some of whom were pensioned by sympathetic kings for their accomplishments. Consider: *Adam Smith* (the father of Capitalism); *Voltaire* (famous French writer who spent his life fighting intolerance); *David Hume*; *Thomas Paine*; *Immanuel Kant*; *Pierre Bayle*; *Benjamin Franklin* (considered the Enlightenment ideal); *Mozart* (who wrote the Magic Flute, which expressed the spirit of the age); *James Madison* (author of the American Constitution); *Jean-Jacques Rousseau* (whose writings greatly influenced the French and American revolutions); *Francis Hutcheson* (one of the founders of the Scottish Enlightenment).

The list goes on. The *Statue of Liberty* in New York Harbor, raising the torch of liberty and knowledge for all to see, was a gift from France meant to represent Enlightenment Age ideals that gave the United States its birth.

These moral and intellectual champions shaped the very best aspects of our liberal culture. We reap their benefits every day.

It was not just these icons of thought and science who made the Enlightenment what it was. Thanks to the printing press, it was the reading masses who swiftly replaced Dark Age superstition with free thought, religious toleration, human rights and dignity, and republican principles of government. Their excitement for life, freedom and discovery contagiously spread across the Western world.

Of course, not everything from that prodigious age has withstood the scrutiny of time. The Enlightenment project of the 17th and 18th centuries, while phenomenal in many ways, was still rooted in the limited knowledge and prejudice of the times. As beneficial as it was, its greatest potential for the future was diverted by material success and never fully realized.

Without this explosive enthusiasm for truth, reason and humanity, Western civilization would still be a collection of competing monarchies wallowing in ignorance and intolerance. Doctors would still be using astrological charts and spells. Education would remain limited to the teachings of Aristotle. We might still be struggling with the issues of slavery and women's suffrage. Belligerent imperialism would continue to mar international relationships with bloodshed. Witches would still be burned at the stake. Free thought, which is the life blood of positive freedom, would be suppressed as radically threatening.

Chivalry-Now recognizes the Enlightenment as a *Kairos* event, a point in time that instigates a significant evolutionary change in consciousness. It was comparable to another Kairos event known as the *Axial Age* (800 – 200 B.C.E.), which produced the Buddha, Lao Tsu, Confucius, Moses, Plato, the Upanishads, Homer, Heraclitus, Archimedes, Elijah, Jeremiah, Deutero-Isaiah, and many other influential figures.

When we draw together the ideals of chivalry with Age of Enlightenment perceptions, our moral base encompasses the entire authenticity of being human. The ideal of goodness is not just something for us to follow. It is something to understand and be part of, so we can better apply our cognitive-moral discipline to the complexities of life. As proponents of the Enlightenment referred to themselves as *"new philosophers,"* the marriage of virtue and reason that Chivalry-Now espouses aims to produce *"new human beings."*

\* \* \*

**The question confronting** us is this: *where do we stand now?*

Yes, the Enlightenment greatly contributed to our Western heritage – but what are we doing with it? Why have we lost that original enthusiasm which so enlivens our experience of life?

Is there nothing left to learn? Have all our problems been solved? Has success taught us to take our ideals for granted? Should we stand idly by while cheap commercialism and corrupt politics degrade them year after year? Has democracy lost its significance, even as non-Western cultures remain inspired by it?

Our knowledge base has grown exponentially since the 18th century, especially in the last hundred years. If anything, this should have bolstered the Enlightenment project's enthusiasm. But something went wrong.

The Enlightenment lost its regenerative power when people channeled their potential for reason away from philanthropic development and focused instead, with tunnel-vision blindness, on personal greed.

As *Francis Hutcheson* (1694 – 1746) pointed out, "reason is only a subservient power to our ultimate determinations..." Without the direction of a strong moral base and a love for positive freedom, our unleashed cleverness leads away from the quest toward something regressive.

The Gilded Age of the late 19th century proved how true that was. Progress and poverty walked hand-in-hand while a small number of ruthless entrepreneurs profited obscenely. Before the New Deal was implemented in the United States, *sixty percent* of Americans lived below the poverty level. Half of those who sought to enlist in the armed services for World War I were considered unfit because they had never seen a doctor. These statistics are worth remembering when nostalgia for the past portrays something more idyllic.

What remained of our idealism was further shaken by the depravity of two World Wars. The senseless killing and destruction revealed the darker side of humanity in no uncertain terms, shaking our belief in human nature to the core. How does one sustain the illusion of being civilized in the face of trench warfare, armored killing machines and systematic genocide? How was it possible that the irrational propaganda of totalitarianism took control of entire nations, leading to the slaughter not of hundreds or thousands, but of millions? These were nothing like the limited battles of previous centuries. They represented a terrible new phenomenon. That human beings were capable of such evil, marching lockstep without conscience or compassion, nullified whatever was left of our ideals. The idea of civilized expectations had vanished, leaving us with a terrifying philosophical void.

People concluded that the nature of humanity must be deeply flawed. What we considered *good* was simply an illusion. Evil remained just below the surface, ready to pounce.

Thinking people found such depravity devastating. Our enlightened civilization, from which we previously took such pride, had simply failed. Even our idea of God seemed deeply flawed.

In their grief and shame, people failed to sufficiently ask *why did all this happen?*

Was human nature really depraved? Could it produce nothing better? Or had our ideals become so compromised by greed and stultifying hubris that we no longer honored the meaning of life by questioning our own direction?

From this low point in our history *existentialism* leapt forth to deliver an uncompromising splash of reality. In light of so much disappointment, it offered a viable means for people to regain their dignity by demanding strict moral and intellectual integrity.

At least it tried.

Many academics, in search of something to believe in, gravitated toward the critiques that existentialism offered. The masses were not so impressed.

Existentialism's call for personal responsibility was taken by many as something dark and pessimistic. It was seen as an admission of guilt that people were not ready to make. This further demonstrated how impotent Western ideals had become. People preferred to look for solace in the advances brought about by assembly-line economics. Materialism gained the image of being reliable and progressive. It distracted people from the threat of dictators, totalitarianism and mass killing. They could relinquish the risks associated with autonomy by surrendering to the appeal of mass commercialism, allowing advertisers to shape and homogenize their lives.

Even today, many people shy away from the responsibility that personal authenticity demands. They dread having to think for themselves, deciding what is right and what is wrong. Rather than looking into their own souls for reference, they prefer to be led, even blindly, by the trivial rewards that commercialism promises. This makes them easy prey for extremist propaganda, which specializes in force-feeding particular values into the minds of the gullible. They would rather embrace the irrational than question things critically.

What they fail to realize is that uncritically following the crowd is what led to the tragedies of both world wars and the rise of totalitarian regimes.

The quest that Chivalry-Now calls for serves as a remedy for this situation – but only one person at a time. When people fear responsibility, what they really fear is engaging the freedom that authenticity demands. They are afraid of living in the here and now, not only because of the risks involved, but because they no longer know how. The culture fails to teach them.

*  *  *

**To facilitate our individual quests**, Chivalry-Now affirms a progression of Western ideals into a code of ethics (the 12 *Trusts*), and encourages a fellowship of support wherever those ideals take root. This is our cultural approach to improving the world we live in, an approach based on freedom, conscience and virtue.

As a source of cultural identity, this code reaches back to ancient times and invites each of us to participate in a quest from which purpose, meaning and value arise. Here we find the seriousness of life that insists that real virtue has to be self-discovered. At its best, it awakens us to the enthusiasm of our own personal *age of reason*.

We live in a world that contradicts the very idealism that defines us. This causes many serious problems, among them a personal discontent that is almost debilitating. Deep in our hearts, we know that in order to do the right thing, to live authentically, we must make the sober choices that responsibility demands. This means taking a stance against the tidal forces of competing, contrary values that false ideologies constantly raise.

The sad thing is, we have to do this alone. The deeper quest represents a solitary process of personal growth. It is individualized according to our personal needs and experience. A fellowship of the quest can certainly help, but every step one takes is decided by the individual. The lessons learned will always be unique, and therefore vitally important in themselves. Here we find the blend of idealism and realism that makes Western civilization unique.

Chivalry-Now is more than just a haphazard mix of various philosophies from the past. It is not enough to see the rationale of freedom and virtue that flows from ancient Greece to modern times. Its power comes from reclaiming the *enthusiasm* and *dedication* that brings such knowledge to life.

In a world of tiresome ideologies, follow-the-herd mentalities, and constant commercial oppression, the direct discovery of, and subsequent relationship to, truth offers an enthusiasm that is difficult to compare. It is like finding a long-hidden treasure that changes your life forever. It provides a sudden liberation from the bonds of ignorance. Such liberation brings not only enthusiasm, but the kind of joy that can only be attained by experiencing life in the here and now. These are the rewards of authentic living.

Reclaiming the past or bowing to a new set of rules is not enough. It never was. The quest experience is made anew with every person who partakes in it. This uniqueness, which molds itself to the individual, is where enthusiasm must originate. If it does not, something is wrong.

Chivalry-Now calls each of us to learn from life directly. The *12 Trusts* provide a catalyst but they must be followed by action, by personal transformation. The quest becomes our personal Odyssey that continually awakens us. In the face of inevitable disappointments, we must continue toward our spiritual goal.

What is that goal?

It is not an end point, but the journey itself. It is the direction we are heading, unique for every person. Simply put, it is the kind of authentic living that only a quest can bring, filled with purpose and meaning, that leaves the world a better place because we were here.

\* \* \*

**The philosophical content** of the Age of Enlightenment arose from the momentum of the Renaissance, which itself was a resurrection of Greco-Roman thought and creativity. The excitement it generated was partly due to reclaiming the momentum of something lost. Its success was generated by a reawakening of something innate and personally fulfilling.

The Enlightenment focused on the potential of the human mind in questioning the world and how it works, especially the status quo. It challenged ignorance and superstition with a sense of purpose that can only be described as *liberating*. Experimentation led to a sudden flood of discoveries, which suggested unlimited potential.

The movement was far from perfect. Enthusiasm sometimes leads to dangerous extremes, as evidenced by the violence of the French Revolution. More often than not, however, it was progressively sound, spreading freedom of thought, religious tolerance and republican ideas throughout the Western world.

The Enlightenment might best be described as a revolution of the soul. To those who responded, the intellectual excitement was irresistibly contagious. Self-educated thinkers like Benjamin Franklin and wealthy elites like Thomas Jefferson joyously indulged themselves in a wide variety of interests, including astronomy, architecture, philosophy, engineering, and agricultural science. Today's vernacular refers to such people as *Renaissance* men and women for their eclectic interests and accomplishments.

Even philosophy changed, becoming more than airy, intellectual conjecture. It tangibly opened doors to freedom, self-determination and human rights. It removed religious and titled hierarchies from seats of power, and replaced them with democratic leanings.

The impressive accomplishments of this movement, our unique inheritance, have unfortunately become so commonplace that we take them for granted. The energy and optimism that they once inspired, and still can, is difficult to appreciate.

Imagine living in a time and place that inhibited, condemned and persecuted free thought and initiative. In feudal societies, you were born into a particular caste and there you stayed. Children, for the most part, were not schooled. People looked to superstition to confront problems like disease and famine. Lower classes were considered the expendable property of their overlord from birth until death. Ignorance made the world a fearful place to live in. As the years went by, nothing seemed to change except for the seasons and the progression to old age – at least for those few who managed to survive.

Suddenly, an idea spreads across the land like wildfire, changing everything. You are permitted and even encouraged to think for yourself and express your opinions. You see a rush of new ideas, discoveries, answers and accomplishments challenging the way things were done before. Transformation is in the air – all due to a focus on reason. The world would never be the same.

Progress was being made in combating disease. Husbandry improved by applying scientific principles. Canals were dug to facilitate commerce. Engines were built to increase productivity. Steel rails eventually stretched across continents, with signals carrying words through simple wire. Universities taught more than just theology and ancient classics. Creativity abounded and the future opened up like never before.

Of course, the Renaissance and Enlightenment did not change things overnight. What facilitated their progress was that a significant number of people were ready for them. There were, of course, those who resisted change, preferring the stability of feudalism. Many in the upper classes viewed change as a threat to their privileges. Nevertheless, once sparked, the inspiration of freedom could not be stopped.

Can we spark such enthusiasm again?

That depends upon our understanding of freedom. Is it just a lack of obvious restraints? Or is it a dynamic that provides the preferred means through which we evolve and bring meaning to the world?

Perhaps we take for granted what no longer exists. Could it be that negative freedom, by itself, propagates a feudal mindset of surrendering to someone else's expectations? Do we look to others for all our answers rather than thinking for ourselves? Are we following our own principles, rooted in Nature's Law? Or do we surrender to prevailing values, no matter how shallow they are, no matter how they contradict each other, for the dubious comfort of fitting in?

To understand the assault upon real Western values to which we are being subjected, just listen to professional propagandists on radio and television. They do not promote discussion or free thought. They use every rhetorical trick to cleverly dictate their own ideological agendas, brazenly confident that a sufficient number of people will sacrifice their own autonomy of thought to believe anything.

That is not the Western way. It does not reflect the genius of antiquity or the Renaissance or the Age of Enlightenment. It silences the call to personal responsibility that echoes from our ancient roots through modern existentialism.

Think about it. How is it that reason, compassion and enlightened self-interest, so central to who we are, are easily ignored? How do we reclaim them in the hope of reclaiming our own integrity?

Despite our wealth of knowledge and advanced technology,

despite the shrinking parameters of the world we live in, and lessons learned at great cost from the Cold War, economic booms and terrible recessions, we find ourselves living in what is rapidly becoming another Dark Age. A new serf mentality has been created, leading the afflicted into a thoughtless compliance with consumerism.

History has given us the tools to know better. We have the knowledge. We have the intellectual pedigree.

What is missing is our will, our self-confidence, our desire to weigh truth against lies when profit or convenience are at stake.

Our loss is not derived from ignorance, although what might be described as a *willful* ignorance is certainly part of it. It comes from feelings of entitled comfort, imaginary fears and a growing predilection toward greed.

Philosopher Andre Compte-Sponville, in his *The Little Book of Atheist Spirituality*, critiqued it best:

"...post-modernity [the times we live in] is modernity *minus the Enlightenment*. It is modernity that has ceased to believe in reason or progress (whether political, social or human) *and thus in itself*. If all value systems are equal, nothing has any value. Science is a myth among others; progress is an illusion; and a democracy respectful of human rights is in no way superior to a society based on slavery and tyranny." (italics mine)

He later added:

"...progress is neither linear nor inevitable... it is [therefore] worth fighting for."

Reason has far greater implications than just a tool used for survival and convenience. It is the source of our nobility that measures and creates who we are.

When Francis Bacon told us that the scientific method was superior to individual genius because it produced results that were more reliable, he did not realize that the method he extolled might someday push individual genius aside, making ignorance tolerable even as technological progress continues to advance. He overlooked that progress, by itself, has no need to be moral. All it requires is interest and method.

What does such amoral progress produce?

A soulless momentum that shamelessly overlooks poverty, willingly bankrupts national economies, and places advanced weapons into the hands of terrorists, knowing full well the possibility that they will someday be aimed at us.

\* \* \*

**We start by** better incorporating the use of reason into our lives. We do that through everyday choices, made manifest by the way we treat other people.

Reason is not just a tool to meet particular needs. That would produce a culture of rote homogeneity. We end up disassociating ourselves from a significant portion of Areté, those qualities that make us exceptionally human.

It is wrong to expect science and technology to carry us forward on their own, without effort on our part. All we have to do is purchase the latest gadget and learn what buttons to push. Such a life surrenders itself to commercial fashion and convenience, which makes us slaves of the marketplace.

This is not to say that we should all become scientists or philosophers. What it means is that authentic living involves a healthy interest in the world we live in. We need to put aside the incessant drone of commercial voices and think for ourselves. There is no other way to imbue our lives with the purpose and meaning that human nature calls for.

As supposedly rational beings of the 21$^{st}$ century, it is amazing how many of us flirt with superstitions, such as astrology or the power of wishful thinking, that make a mockery of our intelligence. We simply ignore the proven genius that made Western culture unique, and replace it with anything that makes us feel good.

We are still living in the post-war, *don't-think-for-yourself-or-question-the-status-quo* mentality. The incurious, *ready to follow anything* mindset has come to dominate a culture that was meant to produce quite the opposite. The popularity of tabloid gossip and undeserved celebrities stands as proof.

Ancient Greeks, who were more in tune with nature than we are today, recognized that rational thought is a strong part of human Areté, the corollary and extension of reflective consciousness that completes our nature. It makes us responsible for the way we live, and for the damage that willful ignorance propagates. Consciousness alone does not complete us. How we utilize that consciousness does.

\* \* \*

**Human beings are** curious by nature. We see this in babies as they fearlessly explore the world around them. Our brains are hardwired to ask questions, find answers, view the world as a challenge to understand. That is how a healthy mind works. The success stories of history bear this out.

Not exercising this potential meaningfully leads to a growing cultural deficit and social malaise.

Why do we do that?

As individuals, we may feel too insecure about our opinions to articulate them meaningfully. Perhaps we never understood the rationale of a personal quest. Perhaps we were intimidated by loudly aggressive or controlling people. We may have identified with the first answers that we heard as children and refuse to consider other possibilities.

I think that a lot of good people merely go with the flow, trusting that problems will be solved by someone else. They end up supporting whatever prejudice or corruption that breeds around them. To compound the problem, the spectacular progress of technology, which Enlightenment thinkers would certainly have appreciated, tends to repress the very spirit that fostered it. We let others do the thinking and creating, while we sit back and enjoy the triviality that comes from it.

We are reminded of Edmund Burke's warning: *"...it is not permitted that we should trifle with our existence."*

Perhaps it is inevitable that something fundamental in human nature will be lost through our own process of development. There are so many people in the world that it is easy to feel insignificant. There are too many conveniences and distractions to choose from – and too few voices crying out in the desert to advocate for something better.

* * *

**Our relationship with reason** has shifted over the centuries. The excitement of the Enlightenment movement brought with it a sense of liberation that was contagious and life-affirming. New discoveries, a populace growing more literate every day, a feeling of integrity and almost unlimited intellectual potential, drew the best from those who embraced it.

As time went on, some of that excitement waned. We became acquainted with the limitations of reason, even as we took progress for granted. With the arrival of assembly-lines, motor vehicles, electronic communications, modern medicine, and home computers, innovation gradually became an anticipated distraction from our own moral and psychological needs. We become, first and foremost, *consumers*.

As technological advancement became obsessively more profitable, the progress of human nature did not keep pace.

Computer games, constant entertainment and meaningless cell phone chatter left little concern for deep thought or inner development. One had to remove oneself in order to find oneself.

The invaluable media soon traded its noble calling for the popularity of gossip and its capacity to appeal to just about every vice – with almost no judgment. This was justified in the name of *freedom* no less – *free enterprise*, the right for each person to make money even if they contributed to the degeneracy of our culture, has become our top priority. The more money that could be made, the more negative freedom was being exploited as somehow more important than positive freedom, even when it produced amoral, or even immoral results. Such freedom provided the excuse for the arms industry to supply advanced weaponry to friend and enemy alike. Whereas freedom was once defined as mature responsibility, it had become a license for greed.

As a culture, we are losing our natural impetus to grow and evolve. The genius of the innovative few has relinquished the need for the rest of us to care about anything beyond our own wants. Today's concern remains far more focused on ease, comfort and entertainment than the experience of life and our own evolution.

Where we once delighted in economic and social progress as a boon to humanity, we now sit back and wait for meaningless innovations. The Information Age, with the Internet opening doors to every thought and interest, and cell phones connecting people every minute of the day, puts everything at our fingertips, while dehumanizing us at the same time. As the rush of science carries us forward, we need to wonder what we left behind.

We need to replace the Information Age with something new, an *Age of Personal Engagement* perhaps, or an *Age of Light* that propagates not only convenience, invention and purchasing power, which can be good in themselves, but Areté as well.

Jesus said it with incredible precision. *What does it profit a man to gain the whole world and lose his soul?*

Reason makes it possible to differentiate between what has value and what cheapens our existence to the point of living-death. It respects truth – and never was there a time more in need of what is true. It can give us the power and self-esteem to pull us away from the trappings of commercialism, and imbue our lives with meaning instead.

Only when enough of us claim the authenticity that reason and virtue make possible, will a new Renaissance begin.

\* \* \*

**During the heyday** of the Enlightenment, the use of reason and science extended itself even into the realm of theology.

As part of an ongoing debate, the famous mathematician, Gottfried Wilhelm Leibniz, concluded that the natural world that God created had to be "the best of all possible worlds." It stood to reason, he thought, that God's perfection would produce nothing less. With that statement, Leibniz believed that the debate was over.

Another philosopher, David Hume, decided to refute that idea. Before long, a controversy raged between two camps: the *traditionalists,* who insisted that God could be found in Scripture, and the *new philosophers,* who pointed to nature as God's direct and perfect revelation. A few, like Bishop Joseph Butler, straddled both sides.

In the midst of that heated debate, there was a terrible earthquake in Lisbon in which thousands of people were killed. Stunned and deeply troubled, theologians and philosophers across the spectrum tried to explain how God could allow such a tragedy. None of their explanations proved satisfying.

The famous French philosopher, Voltaire, was especially moved by the terrible suffering of the Lisbon earthquake. He felt offended by his colleagues' attempts to exonerate the mystery of

God because of it. He considered it so vile that he refused to partake in the speculations, even as he sought the answer in his own conscience. After many years, his contemplations resulted in *Candide*, a satire that, for many, expressed the soul of Enlightenment thinking.

*"Let us cultivate our garden,"* he declared at the end of this strange novella. In those five words, he told us that the purpose of our lives is plainly set, and we should not be distracted from it by sophistry. It is far better to put needless argument aside and work on improving the world as we can.

Our first concern should be to bring an end to suffering and evil.

In this short, literary gem, Voltaire neatly sums up the spirit of the Enlightenment. We should focus on improving the human condition rather than wasting our energies in meaningless debates that do nothing to promote progress.

This incredibly practical idea strongly contributed to the separation of church and state, so that one discipline would no longer hinder or compete with the other. It ended the pogroms and inquisitions and wars of religious intolerance that oppressed free thought. It allowed for us, today, to enjoy the fruits of diversity and interrelationship that contribute so grandly to the cause of peace.

We can waste time wrestling over specifics about truth and God, doctrines and heresy – or we can do the good work that lies before us that does not need fanciful justification. Instead of squabbling over differences in theories or wishful thinking, we can humbly admit that we do not and cannot fully know all there is about truth. It is far better to concentrate on living rightly and loving our fellow human beings. This is how, as Voltaire tells us, we *cultivate our garden,* which is the world we live in.

# Chapter 9

# Nature's Law — *The Fusion of Conscience & Reason*

**The goal of Chivalry-Now is** to heal our Western culture by resurrecting ideals that are vital to us all.

We recognize that this healing is impossible if all we do is exhume a philosophical corpse that has little to do with today's world. Of course it is right to respect wisdom from the past, if only to see how we got to where we are. Human development, however, does not call us to move backwards, or reject what is valid from our new perspectives. It pushes us forward with an obligation for the future.

Medieval chivalry had its time to flourish; so too, ancient philosophies. Although existentialism still has active enthusiasts, it is not the force it once was. Time moves on. Our world is different. *We are different.* Our needs have changed.

We need to reclaim our natural momentum in order to build the next great epoch in human development. That means taking from the past to jump-start the present. It is even possible to learn from the future if we learn to think *prospectively*. Although guidance from a book like this may be helpful, it cannot replace the energy that comes from direct participation.

Our challenge is to liberate ourselves from the constraints of past authorities even as we learn from them. If, for example, we learn something important from the writings of Plato, that knowledge automatically changes as we filter it into our consciousness. It no longer belongs just to Plato. It becomes part of who we are, modified by our own understanding. This makes the quest a living encounter with truth at every moment of one's life.

This relationship with truth, moral truth especially, originates in the depth of our being. It is part of us already. It strives to complete who we are, *because we are incomplete without it.* That includes our sense of right and wrong, which either develops as we grow or atrophies from disuse.

We refer to this sense of right and wrong as *conscience*, an innate recognition of what is good and what is bad. Conscience generates feelings of guilt or satisfaction, depending on our decisions. We sometimes call it *our better angels,* or a still, small voice, or even God trying to tell us something.

That conscience is real is not in question. Direct experience proves that it is. We may not know exactly what it is or how it works, but healthy individuals experience it directly every day.

This is a point of wonder. The fact that conscience exists among psychologically healthy people deserves far more respect than it receives. If it had previously not existed and just suddenly appeared, we would be amazed by its moral implications, its power of discernment, and how it seems part of our own nature.

From such a perspective, we would describe the existence of conscience as an internal moral determinant that borders on the miraculous. It provides convincing evidence that we are inherently moral creatures – or at least we start out that way.

Scholars and philosophers point to conscience as the origin of moral laws and traditions. Theologians like Thomas Aquinas claimed that God's design for human beings included conscience to serve as our moral barometer. Whenever we choose evil over good, we go against that original nature from which, as his religious perspective saw it, we are fallen.

Conscience by itself, however, is incomplete. It is not enough to feel pangs of guilt now and then, or be moved by philanthropic interest. We need to recognize the complexities of what is good and bad in order to fulfill our moral inclinations.

That requires that conscience be supplemented by intelligence and reason.

The important relationship between conscience and reason is recognized in the history of jurisprudence, which refers to it as *Nature's Law* – the natural, moral impulse that provides the basis for civil law. This coincides with the Areté of human nature, where reason, virtue and compassion comprise the highest good.

Thomas Jefferson thought the concept so important that he mentioned it prominently in the Declaration of Independence as the *Laws of Nature and of Nature's God*. From his Age of Enlightenment perspective, he proudly declared that certain truths and rights derived from these laws were *unalienable* and *self-evident*.

In later writings, Jefferson elaborated:

"Nature has written her moral laws on the head and heart of every rational and honest man, where man may read them for himself. If ever you are about to say anything amiss, or to do anything wrong, consider beforehand [that] you will feel something within you which will tell you it is wrong, and ought not to be said or done. This is your conscience, and be sure and obey it... Conscience is the only sure clue which will eternally guide a man clear of all his doubts and inconsistencies."

Please note how he says that Nature's Laws were written not only in the *heart* but in the *head* as well, pointing out the strong connection between conscience and reason. Conscience provides *the only sure clue* that will *guide a man clear of all his doubts*.

Jefferson's political nemesis, Alexander Hamilton, seemed to concur:

"The sacred rights of mankind are not to be rummaged for among old parchments or musty records. They are written, as with a sunbeam, in the whole volume of human nature, by the hand of the divinity itself."

Centuries earlier, Aristotle suggested that human virtue was not imposed from without, but blossomed from within. Unimpeded by error or distraction, people feel a natural affinity toward ideas of fairness, human rights and equality. We know the difference between right and wrong in our hearts, no matter how imperfectly, which reason should use as its foundation. This ancient insight struck a philosophical chord in Western culture that has resonated ever since.

The only way to understand Nature's Law is to experience it directly. As Hamilton said, it is not a compilation of rules or regulations, or the result of commandments carved in stone or otherwise. It is not related to the concrete, mathematical view of deductive science, as would be Newton's law of gravity.

Nature's Law is the integration of reason with an intuitive moral proclivity that completes a person's consciousness and character. We refer to the integration and activation of these qualities as *authenticity*.

The convergence of reason and conscience recognizes the dignity of human rights and moral principles. Those who fail to integrate or utilize Nature's Law remain incomplete, not fully engaged with life as a quest for growth and moral understanding.

Through Nature's Law we can apply our sense of justice, fairness and compassion in our everyday lives. Civil laws are made in response to this.

John Locke, the Enlightenment philosopher who most influenced Jefferson, believed that acting dishonorably meant acting against nature. He said that the moral equality of human beings is based on their having a *shared commonality of being* (or as Jefferson later put it, "all men are created equal"). Nature's Law is what steers people toward the common good, and away from being mired in self-interest. Personal ethics are more than social niceties. They are duties we have toward others by virtue of our being human. Simply put, as social creatures it is our nature to be concerned with one another's well-being. When we fail to be concerned about our neighbor, something is wrong and needs attention.

John Locke deeply believed this:

"To take away wrongfully from another and for one man to advance his own interest by the disadvantage of another man is more contrary to nature than death, than poverty, than pain, than any other evil."

While the ancients saw natural law as the obligation to act justly, Enlightenment thinkers came to a slightly different conclusion. They claimed that there were *actual human rights*. Treating people well should not be viewed as an act of magnanimity. It is behavior that everyone should naturally adhere to. People have certain rights, and we are obligated to respect them.

Seeing how I keep dipping into the past for references to Nature's Law, one might wonder if it were still relevant today. Has our more extensive understanding of the natural world made it irrelevant?

Earlier generations certainly viewed the world differently than we do. Despite their fascination with the scientific method, their understanding of nature was only in the early stages. This made them susceptible to error.

Even so, their more intuitive approach to knowledge offers much to consider.

For one thing, their frame of mind was that of a liberated *explorer,* which prepares one well for the requirements of a quest. They were open to insights and discoveries that cannot be found in the classroom. They approached things not only objectively but subjectively, which demands a measure of personal intuition and investment – exactly what the objective scientist seeks to avoid. If the quest tells us anything it is that our experience of life cannot be separated from our study of it. How can we remove ourselves from our own inquiry? Why should we? Objectivity is only part of our encounter with the world, a part that consciousness automatically makes subjective. We are part of every equation. Questions cannot exist without people to articulate them.

Oddly enough, quantum physics says pretty much the same.

There are invaluable insights derived from the intuitive mind that cannot be found in the laboratory or the classroom. Why? Because it taps into the hidden reservoir of the sub-conscious, of which the conscious mind is unaware.

The point is this: There is much to be said for having a direct confrontation with Mystery in our lives. It breeds an authenticity that draws us into sharp experience of the moment, which is life-expanding. Purposeful exploration and discovery become a steady process that defines who we are in relationship to the world. It differentiates between those who are awake in the here and now, and those who are not.

There are other aspects of subjectivity to consider. Consider the act of *knowing,* which is a direct, subjective experience in time, compared to *knowledge,* which is a collection of facts, like a database, available when needed, but not expressive in itself. *Knowing* something to be true is an active state of mind, a mindful affirmation made rich by personal awareness.

Consider how intuition helps us recognize bits and pieces of truth with jarring excitement when we come across them. What about dreams, and archetypal images that express knowledge subconsciously? These are all valid experiences that expand the limited capacity of our minds.

In no way do I intend to deny the scientific method its invaluable due. Science remains a tremendously valuable asset to our growth and survival as a species. I only point out that there are other approaches to learning that have unique value of their own. They not only enhance our understanding of the world, they contribute to personal growth as well.

When we limit our approach to knowledge or fail to respect different kinds of experience, we can expect repercussions. For one thing, we fall into a dependency that hampers personal initiative. Something is lost when we find ourselves completely dependent on teachers, experts and media talking heads for our opinions. When we adopt ready-made answers as our own, we severely limit our experiential involvement. This cookie-cutter, conveyor belt mentality fashions a very different relationship with truth than our questing ancestors enjoyed. We become passive recipients rather than explorers, protagonists, or heroes who confront life with enthusiasm. We passively accept what is given to us, or allow bias to choose on our behalf. For me, that is only half-living.

Let me say this more directly. We know in our hearts when the fullness of direct involvement is missing in our lives, despite all the conveniences, distractions and knowledge at our fingertips. We suffer from a lack of balance, a lack of connection. We not only sense it, *we know it as well*. We are frustrated because of it.

Too many of us have become intellectually lazy. Our complex lives have turned us into specialists who focus on minor, everyday issues without seeing what is around us. Why not be generalists for whom the world is open for constant review?

Be aware of how commercialism has veered society away from building individual *persons* in order to shape us into *consumers* – a word suggesting herds of obedient shoppers waiting in line with shopping carts overflowing, dutifully consuming more than they produce. When that happens, an integral part of who we are is left to decay. Our nature, which yearns for the quest to help us learn and grow, is sadly ignored.

Enlightenment philosophers experienced the discovery and gathering of knowledge as an exciting, integral part of their quests, a source of wonder and reverence. What greater relationship to truth could be had than acquiring and expanding their knowledge of it, and then using that knowledge to create a better world? They told us that this is where real nobility could be found, rather than in bloodlines or decadent, aristocratic titles. This is our highest calling from which our full potential arises. It is our truest conduit for purpose and meaning.

Unfortunately, the enthusiasm of Enlightenment ideals has waned over the last two centuries. Taking a more intelligent, proactive role in shaping our own evolution has lost its appeal. We have receded from that path, and suffer culturally because of it.

We are told in a hundred ways to memorize prefabricated and crippling ideologies that are conveniently mired in the status quo (what I sometimes call the *stagnant quo*). Trusting someone else's imperfect reasoning over our own, we surrender to a group identity, hoping to find the security and comfort of belonging. That alone squelches our potential, reducing freedom to a slavish, uninspired submission that leads nowhere.

That does not include everyone, of course. There are always those who observe and evaluate life directly and form their own opinions. They naturally stand out from the *stagnant quo*. You see it in their eyes, sense it in their words and personal energy. They provide examples of humanity trying to assert itself positively once again.

Two different mindsets exist – one dependent, unimaginative and obsessed by self-interest, devaluing knowledge as a tool for personal gain or pleasure, or just for getting by. The other is notable for its independent thought, for appreciating the deeper meaning of life, for recognizing real virtue and dedicating one's life to the greater good.

\* \* \*

**What should we do?**
Because of the environment we live in, burdened by consumerist values and the never-ending combat between liberal and conservative extremes, it is up to us, as well-meaning individuals, to

preserve and defend the best of our cultural inheritance. In order to keep that wisdom alive and relevant, we need to incorporate what is new at the same time. Nature's Law, with its fundamental base of reason and conscience, supports that conclusion.

We find the existence of moral and social law in all societies, despite cultural differences. This is no accident. It reflects the moral conscience of human nature itself. When certain mammalian instincts began expressing themselves in the distant past through rational thought, it was only natural for common values to develop over time. As primitive thought continued to develop, moral tendencies became clear and a full-blown rational conscience made its debut. Written laws reflect that process.

The utility that comes from Nature's Law is not given to us whole-cloth from the moment of our birth. It gains ascendency as we mature. It places us in direct relationship with the mystery of life and existence itself. It grows as we grow, and as our ability to reason becomes more refined. Properly utilized, it flourishes; neglected, it shrivels into suppressed feelings of discontent. Just as a seed requires water and nourishment to grow, the mind requires independent thought and deep reflection for its full potential to blossom.

The mind that ignores conscience is diverted from its natural growth. Ready-made answers make it lazy. Submission to peer pressure or social expectations ruins its autonomy. A passive commitment to the mundane closes doors to inspiration. All these traps inhibit us from partaking in our ideals.

Included in these traps is a poverty of love and passion.

Our view of ethics depends upon our view of human nature in relationship to the world we live in. However we define our values, they define us in return. It is imperative not to leave that process to chance, external coercion or expediency.

\* \* \*

**Nature's Law lends itself** well to philosophy and the cause of jurisprudence.

But what about religion?

In the Declaration of Independence, Jefferson referred to the *Laws of Nature and of Nature's God,* as if they were identical.

The wording is typical of Enlightenment philosophers. Most of them approached the idea of God through reason, a method commonly referred to as *deism.* This allowed them to speak of God in non-sectarian terms that would be relevant to all religions and to freethinkers as well. Thomas Jefferson was a deist, as was Benjamin Franklin. Many of the founders of the United States, while not deists in the proper sense, shared similar sympathies. Some, like John Adams, were Unitarians. Others, like Samuel Adams and John Jay, were dedicated Christians. Despite these differences, they worked together for religious tolerance and a benign separation of church and state. To assure this unity, they went so far as to keep the word *God* out of the Constitution, even though most, if not all of them, believed in some sort of deity.

We can therefore assert that Nature's Law should be compatible with all faiths, and with Christian thought in particular. I will focus on Christianity because it remains the most popular and influential religion in the West. (In order to keep our doors open to everyone, Chivalry-Now does not endorse any particular religion, nor cast aspersions on atheism or agnosticism. Our mission is to support virtues that are common to us all.)

In the Ten Commandments, the latter seven (depending on how you count them) refer to social morality and reflect the very essence of Nature's Law. So does the Golden Rule of Jesus, telling us to love our neighbor as ourselves.

*St. Paul* affirmed Nature's Law quite specifically in his letter to the Romans, chapter 2, verses 14, 15:

"When Gentiles who do not have the law do by nature what the law requires, they are a law unto themselves, even though they do not have the law. They show that what the law requires is written on their hearts, while their conscience also bears witness…"

From this perspective, we could easily conclude that Jesus was trying to incorporate Nature's Law as part of his mission. This can be seen from his own New Testament references to truth, new birth and how the written law condemns a man, but the *new law* gives him life. In Hebrews, when Paul reminds us that the Spirit will write the law of God in people's *hearts and minds*, he might as well be saying *conscience and reason*. The meanings are interchangeable.

Church doctor, Thomas Aquinas, considered Nature's Law as the way that people connect and participate in God's *Eternal Law*. The use of reason is what makes this connection possible. It is our moral obligation to seek and support what is good, while at the same time resisting what is evil.

The words of Jesus, who was highly respected by most Enlightenment deists, boiled it down to terms that are honored for their simplicity:

"'Love the Lord your God with all your heart and with all your soul and with all your mind.' This is the first and greatest commandment. And the second is like it: 'Love your neighbor as yourself.' All the Law and the prophets hang on these two commandments." Mathew 22: 37-40

*Heart, soul and mind* – once again, we see the telling formula of conscience and reason. His last sentence stresses that *"All the Law and prophets hang on these two commandments."* There it is. The written law is dependent on what Jefferson later called "The Laws of Nature and Nature's God."

If we contemplate this, a whole new world of meaning opens up, which just happens to reflect the very heart of our living quest.

This sheds light on another quote of Jesus: *"The truth will set you free."* This tells us that true freedom comes from a state of authentic living that brings truth into our lives. *Positive freedom.* In comparison, the inauthentic life is not free at all, but an aimless slavery mired in its own stagnation.

Jesus also tells us that we need to be *"born again"* in order to be complete – akin to a transformational process that might be comparable to anagnorisis. Like Nicodemus, we ask *how?* The answer is clear. When we reclaim our full moral selves it results in new awareness, and from new awareness a *new and more complete creation* is born. When conscience and reason combine, falsehood and illusion show exactly what they are. Consciousness is enhanced by what Jesus described as new and more abundant life.

This might explain how the *kingdom of God* can be present and yet not be seen by those who are "deceived." It is a matter of perception – opening one's mind and heart to see a greater truth.

In Chivalry-Now we refer to this state of mind as *Grail Consciousness*, an integral part of experiencing life as a quest through which we claim our true moral identities. Nature's Law makes it clear that a fusion of conscience and reason awakens us to authenticity.

# Chapter 10

# Existentialism — *Freedom & Responsibility*

**Philosophers have a way** of taking ideas that are profoundly simple and making them so abstract that the average reader fails to appreciate them. To make things worse, professors tend to focus on those very abstractions rather than teaching common sense applications. The important lessons are overlooked due to pedantry, limiting philosophy to school curriculums.

*Existentialism* has suffered from this very problem. Even as it remains highly respected in academia, the general public knows little about it.

Most of us dread having to read the works of Sartre or Camus or Heidegger – and for good reason. Their writing styles are slow and ponderous compared to modern expectations. Sartre's fixation on *essence* versus *existence* is more of a conundrum for pseudo-intellectuals than anything meaningful for our daily lives. Most people are just not interested.

To avoid this problem, let us now go to the heart of the matter. The core principle of existentialism is simply this: *personal responsibility*.

We cannot escape the fact that, as human beings living in a complex world, we are faced with making choices every day. These choices define who we are. They give us opportunities to assert our preferences and values in the way we live. In this respect, they provide the means through which we become more complete and consciously alive.

The Enlightenment project of the 17th and 18th centuries introduced a new appreciation of human nature based on our capacity for reason. Unfortunately, the project was never completed. While it set the stage for a new and progressive outlook on life, its potential to expand reason and virtue reached its zenith and then sadly declined. What replaced it was a by-product of its success, the priority of wealth and power. Post-Enlightenment intellectuals were convinced that material progress was the truest measurement showing that humanity was still on the right track.

For an aggressive and often ruthless minority, the riches gained during America's *Gilded Age* (in contrast to the *Golden Age* of ancient Greece) seemed to prove this. While Thomas Jefferson's words about *equality* were quoted in speeches and history books, they were being disregarded in the real world. Before long, capitalism spilled beyond the narrow field of economics and became a malformed caricature of moral ethics, which saturates Western culture even today. The teachings of Adam Smith were soon measuring the value not only of trade but of everyday relationships. Philanthropy and goodwill now had to compete with the bartering-mentality of the marketplace. The positive freedom associated with the quest was replaced by the structured dynamics of free enterprise. Greed became respectable as it more and more defined who we are.

Jefferson had warned us about this decades earlier:

"Greediness for wealth, and fantastical expense, have degraded, and will degrade, the minds of our citizens. These are the peculiar vices of commerce. The selfish spirit of commerce knows no country, and feels no passion or principle but that of gain."

To substantiate what was happening, Darwin's theory of evolution was wrongly exploited to aggrandize the success of certain business moguls. *Social Darwinism* claimed that successful people were higher on the evolutionary scale, and deserved special rights and privileges. They were not bound by the same rules and values that governed everyone else.

This mirrored the aristocratic attitude of the medieval mindset. It flew in the face of Enlightenment liberalism by justifying a huge and growing disparity between rich and poor. In the United States, business elites constructed private palaces that rivaled those of Europe. At the same time, poverty spread across the land. This was not to change until the New Deal

The morality of the Enlightenment and of altruistic Christianity, would be shocked by this development. Gilded Age morality justified itself by insisting that each person got what he or she deserved, no matter what the circumstances. As greed took greater hold, it defiled what was left of our higher ideals.

* * *

**Modern existentialism was born** somewhat later out of the carnage and philosophical collapse brought about by the devastation of two World Wars.

Prior to that, European culture took pride in its self-image and material accomplishments. It considered itself humane, advanced and civilized – the epitome of cultural advancement constantly heading in the right direction. They justified their actions by saying that their economic and intellectual achievements would eventually eliminate both poverty and international conflict, even though their immediate aim had more to do with their own bank accounts.

They were completely unprepared for the savage inhumanity that lay just below the surface. They failed to realize that their modern civilization was little more than a façade designed to make personal and corporate greed palatable. Material success had blinded them to deeply human values that were being lost.

Competition for economic supremacy, fueled by nationalistic pride, suddenly unleashed a conflict of technological violence and inhumanity that the world had never seen before.

The first World War, with its machine guns, mustard gas,

trench warfare, aerial attacks and huge number of casualties, shook the foundations of Western culture. That such incredible slaughter and destruction had been perpetrated for no other reason than to see which nation would gain economic supremacy quickly shattered the illusion of benign social values. Greed had accomplished its subversive work. As the shadow-side of human nature raised its ugly head, no one could stop the insanity that followed.

In the dazed aftermath, while disillusioned populations struggled to understand what happened and why, World War II quickly followed, carrying the depravity to even greater extents. Submarine attacks upon civilian vessels, the swift mechanizations of blitzkrieg, mass bombings of populated cities, state-controlled systematic genocide, and the most singular harbinger of death, the atom bomb, all pointed to human nature as the epitome of evil.

People no longer knew what to believe. All the illusions of progress and security that they once cherished had been obliterated in the worst possible ways. The reverse morality of Friedrich Nietzsche, who considered liberal democracy a failed experiment, suddenly seemed vindicated. The Enlightenment ideals of freedom, rational thought and ownership of property were being rejected by those who feared that these would somehow lead to authoritarian takeovers. Liberal contrivances, like Franklin D. Roosevelt's New Deal, were quickly set up in order to save capitalism and protect democracies from the communist revolutions that assailed Eastern Europe and Asia.

Without proper answers and a clear vision of direction, there arose a reactionary distrust of all things civilized that can still be found in political extremism. Sigmund Freud lent an intellectual veneer to this negativity by explaining that human beings are naturally prone to instincts of violence. He insisted that by repressing those instincts civilization only made them worse. In contrast to Nietzsche, Freud sought not to liberate those darker instincts, but to find better ways of controlling them. The battered insecurity of Europe's post war intelligentsia mildly accepted his ideas.

Voices of reason, equally discouraged, went silent. It appeared that Western civilization was about to lose everything about it that was unique and good. The vision of Locke, Voltaire and Jefferson was being replaced by those of Nietzsche, Freud and Marx.

As people surrendered to Freud's psychological determinism, a small minority boldly resisted. Still believing in the values of freedom and personal responsibility, they resisted the defeatism and paranoia that was replacing them.

Jean-Paul Sartre, the man most associated with existentialism, was one of them. He wrote the following opening line in one of his articles:

*"What can be said from the very beginning is that by existentialism we mean a doctrine which makes human life possible..."*

At face value, this is a startling claim. It infers that human life is more than just a human body that is by chance alive. The authentic human life is not produced solely by an act of birth. It is a *possibility* that needs to be developed. We need some sort of code or doctrine in order to activate our full potential.

Existentialism sheds light on how to achieve that.

It taught that human nature must never be thought of as the sum of Freud's determinism and Nietzsche's obsession with power. To complete itself, human nature must rise above all that. It attains its purest dignity, purpose and destiny through a firm grasp of freedom, compassion and responsibility. We do not have to ask some psychoanalyst, philosopher or guru to explain that. We know it in our hearts and minds because it is part of who we are. We feel its deep yearning to express itself.

The authentic human being is someone who engages life with

a full acceptance of personal responsibility. We define this responsibility as the *ability to respond* to life with truth, justice, integrity and compassion. We recognize our moral choices in everything we do. When we face them boldly, we actualize who we are in the process. This is what separates us from Freud's deterministic conclusions. There is always more to us than psychoanalysis can explain.

Areté fails if we abdicate this responsibility in order to follow the crowd, or surrender to the ready-made taglines of political ideologies, or to prejudices that stop the moral process right in its tracks. Areté is achieved when we consistently use our capacity for intelligent compassion, accepting the risks that come from that, while respecting the primacy of truth overall.

What Existentialism manages to provide is a proper response to the untimely failure of the Enlightenment. In some respects, it carries the project forward in order to complete it.

* * *

**Experiencing the Nazi** occupation of France during World War II, Sartre saw examples of the worst side of human nature. He saw German soldiers commit unspeakable atrocities, shutting off their own moral dictates in the name of nationalistic pride. (In their later defense, they offered the poorest excuse of all, "I was just following orders.") He also saw French collaborators betraying their own countrymen out of fear or to win favor. He concluded, and stated so in no uncertain terms, that *evil flourishes directly from moral cowardice*. We are completely accountable for all that we do.

Sartre rejected the excuses of soldiers and collaborators unequivocally. He insisted that each person is responsible for his or her actions down the line. Our decisions make us who we are. The decision to comply with evil, or not resist it, is a decision that robs us of our humanity – not just as individuals, but as a society.

Here was the piece of the Enlightenment project that 19<sup>th</sup> century greed had managed to suppress.

Reason is capable of leading people out of ignorance and barbarity, and can produce incredible benefits for us all. But *reason is not enough*. The miracles of progress do not release us from the moral obligations to make freedom work as a proper expression of human nature. Instead, they produce hubris under false pretenses.

The leaders of the Enlightenment understood that human authenticity was inseparable from virtue. Without the self-discipline of virtue, reason becomes a double-edged sword, quite capable of world wars, genocide, atomic bombs, authoritarian regimes, and the kind of cowardice that relinquishes one's own humanity for momentary gain. The moral blindness that conflicting values produce, gave birth to monstrous enemies of life. If it were not for the support of moral cowards, Hitler, Stalin and so many other tyrants would never have come into power.

\* \* \*

**After World War II,** all the wisdom of the past seemed morally inadequate. People did not know what to believe anymore. Reason appeared to have failed them completely. Nationalism was far too risky. Religion was judged impotent against the backdrop of the Holocaust and Hiroshima. Political leaders could not be trusted, if only for their fallibility. Propaganda had so easily swayed the masses that people did not know what to think anymore.

What remained was appalling. Among the charred remains of European cities, human dignity became nothing more than an illusion. Integrity was sold to the highest bidder. Friends betrayed friends. Conscience became a weak and disposable commodity. As a cheap semblance of morality became more commercialized, it disconnected itself from Nature's Law. "Do unto others as you would have them do unto you," seemed too simplistic for a life principle, even naïve.

People vaguely understood that the atrocities of Hitler and Stalin did not arise in a vacuum. The stage had been set for their rise to power. Despite economic progress, Western ideals had been in steady decline, weakening society at its core. *There was no longer a shared social conscience to serve as a failsafe.* Individuality, while not entirely erased, was being systematically subdued by a strong, commercial pressure to conform. Greed had quietly subverted all our ideals, robbing them of their inspiration when we needed them most.

Existentialism did its best to turn that around. It insisted that we had to resist evil or be labeled as cowards. It called for the kind of courage of which human dignity is made.

Dignity is not a gift that just falls from the sky, or given to us by accident of birth. It comes from *who we make of ourselves*. The *1st Trust* of Chivalry-Now says this plainly: "I will develop my life for the greater good."

Because each of us is ultimately responsible for our behavior, there are no excuses for corrupt decisions, moral slacking, cooperating with evil, or remaining silent in the face of outrage.

Neither can we shirk responsibility by quietly following the crowd, or juggling opposing values as if they were somehow compatible. These are the choices of the coward and the lazy.

Today's citizen needs to understand that the *freedom* we so cherish is not a thing to be grasped, sold or borrowed. The truth is, freedom does not even exist until it is utilized – *and even then only responsibly.* A person may call himself free, but if he lacks *free thought*, he is a slave to habit, or popular opinion, or lethargy, or prejudice, or a convenient lack of conscience. All this detracts from human integrity.

Existentialism looked at the devastation of World War II, the genocidal death camps, and the moral despair that followed, and shouted out to anyone who would listen: *Wake up! Do you want to reclaim dignity that you can believe in? Then stand up and make dignified decisions in everything you do!*

*Do not blame this horror on the happenstance of war. These wars happened because we were living half-lives that were always teetering on moral collapse. The wars did nothing but show us what we had become. When greed destroys compassion, when peer pressure supersedes reason and individuality, when people dutifully follow the crowd and fill their minds with propaganda, disaster is unavoidable.*

The parallels with today are frightfully obvious.

I am reminded of the 2008 Great Recession, and the 2010 oil spill in the Gulf of Mexico. Before they happened, everyone happily lived their lives with blinders on, pushing the acceptability of greed a little further every day. The risks were plain and yet good people convinced themselves that fate would never turn against them. It was clear that the economy could not continue like it was – generating fantastic wealth for those who shuffled electronic exchanges, while manufacturing fell by the wayside. Likewise, the enormous risk of drilling into an underground ocean of poisonous fuel a mile below the ocean's surface was obvious as well. We did not need a catastrophe to know that strict precautionary regulations were necessary and had to be respected.

Instead of using reasonable caution, we merrily danced along on faith alone, the egotistical faith that blindly believed we were so favored by God or destiny that we did not have to worry about consequences. We somehow deserved divine protection, despite all evidence to the contrary, and were more than willing to allow stupidity and greed to prove us right. As long as it increased profits, we brazenly concluded that truth, honor and safety were expendable.

Greed is a slippery slope. We scarcely notice how it draws us further and further away from our own moral dictates until it is too late.

Western nations experienced this moral blindness prior to

World War I, and replaced it with a moral numbness that paved the way for World War II.

Despite all the terrible lessons, we are taking even greater risks today in our tepid response to global warming. It seems that we have learned nothing but how to shut down conscience even more than we did before.

In the events leading up to our recent economic collapse, Wall Street traders and big oil CEOs were committed to generating wealth beyond anyone's need, no matter what the cost to others. They threw caution to the wind. The rest of us, busy with our own greedy routines, said nothing. Accepting the *Big Lie of Consumerism*, we unheroically ignored the problems as if we had no responsibility to do otherwise. We believed whatever the leaders of industry and politics told us.

*Surely they wouldn't lie*, we told ourselves. *The risk would be as great for them as it is for us!*

But they did lie. They risked everything as if the economy, the environment and people's lives were nothing more than plastic chips at a roulette table.

Existentialism is quick to indict this kind of willful ignorance and complacency. It says that *each of us* is not only responsible for ourselves, but for defining through our actions *the rest of humanity as well*. The power of choice was in our hands from the very beginning. The depravity that causes war, that risks the environment and ignores poverty, that feeds bigotry and places profit before everything else, is something we can choose to reject.

Hopefully we will, before it is too late.

\* \* \*

**The philosophers of ancient Greece** awakened the Western soul to the importance of freedom and a meaningful engagement with the world around us. As stated before, they told us that the combination of reason and virtue is what makes us human.

Medieval chivalry gave us an ethical outline of ideals that we distilled into the *12 Trusts*. It introduced us to the quest, which encourages us to encounter life as a learning experience, while exemplifying the virtues that we believe in.

The Enlightenment project of the 17$^{th}$ and 18$^{th}$ centuries gave us a perspective of the world based on reason that was meant to free us from ignorance and superstition. More than anything in a thousand years, it shaped the characteristics of the modern mind.

Responding to a perversion of these ideals, and to the pessimism of post-war Europe, existentialism awakened people to embrace their responsibilities as true individuals, even as commercialism worked its hardest to merge them into bland conformity.

Chivalry-Now traces its lineage from the warrior and philosophical traditions of antiquity, through their refinement in the Middle Ages, and into the Age of Enlightenment. Through existentialism, it finds powerful resonance that refuses to gloss over evil and cowardice. It is a philosophy that promotes strength of character, which is really all that we can ever own.

It teaches us how to enhance reality through our own good efforts. We start by finding and nurturing the ideals already inside us.

\* \* \*

**Reason without compassion** and responsibility separates us from Nature's Law. It separates us from conscience, which is an essential part of human nature. We fall short of our own humanity without it. Reason, by itself, is only a mental process of thought and association.

Without a strong connection with conscience and reason, and the natural result of them both, responsibility, we are subjected to a lack of meaning and direction that pulls us away from authenticity. The result? Our resistance to illusion becomes weak. Truth becomes devalued. We feel comfortable choosing among falsehoods for what appeals to us most. We distract ourselves from our discontent instead of making necessary changes for growth. We tolerate contradictory values until they all seem valid. Before we know it, nothing makes sense anymore. Once we surrender to extreme relativism, the quest escapes us entirely

In light of this failing, existentialism cries out for the sanity of conscience with shocking and often brutal clarity. It reminds us that the direct awakening of self brings affirmation to our own existence.

Existentialists call this confrontation with life *subjectivity*.

When we achieve subjectivity in our lives, we become people who add our own measure of virtue and conscience to the universe itself. And while the universe may seem to be indifferent, our struggle to make sense of things and to instill virtue influences and changes the world in which we live. We become living advocates of Nature's Law, which applies reason to moral awareness, and brings them to life. This is who we are at our finest – our truest source of dignity. The world always reflects our efforts, be they good or bad.

Consider this quote taken from the movie *Excalibur*:

*"When a man lies, he murders some part of the world."*

Here, the character Merlin recognizes the moral consequences of cause and effect that may start out as insignificant, but either feeds into or denies the momentum around it.

Sometimes we find it expedient to lie. It may shield us from punishment, or get us something that we want. Sometimes it is a weapon to use against others. In political strategy, falsehood is used to malign people's characters, turning the democratic process into a farce by exploiting fear and prejudice. Lies have the power to shape the world we live in just as much as truth does, *but in the wrong direction.*

We are constantly faced with choosing one way over the other.

We risk social insanity by tepidly choosing both.

\* \* \*

**The subjectivity of existentialism** includes a deep awareness of life, of being so engaged in living for the moment that it produces a high level of authenticity. This involves not only reason and conscience, but *passion* as well.

In passion we find our personal engine of Areté, the expression of human dignity reminiscent of the Enlightenment's burst of inspiration. The authenticity that comes from it is nothing less than continual growth derived from direct experience. This is what the quest is all about.

During medieval times, and throughout the Age of Reason, personal responsibility was a given. Honor was everything. Explanations of what that meant were not needed.

Things have changed. We have been told that freedom is an economic tool, or the benefit of a particular form of government, instead of something that blossoms with purpose and meaning from inside. True freedom is not something given to us by law or a constitution or a bill of rights. It is a response to life that emanates from our own completeness.

It is important to understand that as valuable as freedom is, it is *not, nor ever should be,* our final goal. Freedom is the *means* to that goal, which is an authentic life that lives up to its moral obligations.

The problem with ideologies that lean toward libertarianism is that they stop at freedom's doorstep, convinced that they have reached their goal. They fail to open the door and move beyond. They measure everything according to an idea of liberation that is aimless, pointless, self-centered, and sometimes morally questionable. They fail to activate their moral centers, which is what the real authenticity that freedom offers is all about. Thinking themselves *arrived*, the cold dissection and measurements of freedom that follow stop them in their tracks.

If we are passionate about truth, if we are free enough to make commitments to others, if our sense of conscience is alive and given form by reason, then the responsibility that existentialism speaks of is not a chore that we should force upon others. It is our natural state. The social contract comes from the aggregate of such people.

Life becomes our passion when we are authentically alive. We are not organic robots. We become part of the herd only when we surrender our autonomy – which existentialism rightly calls cowardice. Enlightenment thinkers would never consider such a surrender. They found the world that they passionately confronted too exciting.

Unfortunately, because it dismissed so many of our mundane illusions and demanded self-accounting, existentialism was seen by many as something dark and pessimistic. Its realism was too demanding for passionless souls who preferred drifting aimlessly with the crowd. For them, responsibility was seen as more of a threat or burden than a virtuous outpouring of life's zeal.

\* \* \*

**Existentialists see the world** around them and resist the urge to fill it with misleading lies.

As temporal beings looking for purpose and meaning in a seemingly amoral universe, we are set up for disappointment. Because of this, one might rightly assume that our position in the universe is fundamentally absurd. We feel abandoned and search for solace wherever we can find it. For all our trouble, all we get back is the echo of our own dismay.

This is, indeed, a dark and frightening vision, a perspective capable of seeing Hitler's death camps, leveled cities, traitorous countrymen and mushroom clouds for what they are. It is no wonder that those who were looking for reassuring illusions considered existentialism a pessimistic and even frightful philosophy. What they failed to see is that *the admission of life's absurdity is where the redemptive process begins*. The problem has to be faced and seen for what it is in order to remedy it.

Life as we see it *is* absurd. It often seems that there is no other way to look at the world and conclude otherwise.

*But that does not mean that we have to be absurd as well.*

Here we find the life-affirming crux of existentialism, the challenge, not unlike the quest, that leads to the integrity and the joy of authentic living.

We are called upon to bring purpose and meaning into our lives by taking life seriously. The onus of freedom falls directly upon the individual, exactly where it should be – not for the sake of license or hedonism, for it rejects both, but for the sake of responsibility, which completes our moral nature to the core. In a sense, we are being tested by our innermost core.

Articulating this, existentialism offers an interesting twist to the Golden Rule. Instead of saying "do unto others as you would have them do unto you," it widens the proposition. We are to ask to determine if our actions would be acceptable for everyone in the world to perform in exactly the same way. After all, as human beings, our behavior adds to the definition of our entire species. What we want that definition to be is part of our every decision. Every day, in everything we do, we contribute to that meaning.

Sartre declared in no uncertain terms that we are responsible not only for who we are, but *who we plan to be*. Only by taking an active role in deciding our personal development can true liberation be found.

A few of his quotes illustrate this:

*"...existentialism's first move is to make every man aware of what he is and to make the full responsibility of his existence rest on him. And when we say that a man is responsible for himself, we do not only mean that he is responsible for his own individuality, but that he is responsible for all men."*

*"Man is nothing else but what he makes himself."*

*"There is not a single one of our acts which does not at the same time create an image of man as we think he ought to be."*

Sartre's view rejects the tendency to surrender to the way things are. No power is capable of enslaving us more than our own cowardice, complacency and lack of judgment. *We are always in a position to resist evil in some manner.* If humanity is to represent anything meaningful at all, we must resist evil. This is how we challenge the absurdity of our own existence. Here we find what we might call the moral impetus of today's knight-errant, the autonomous warrior of the quest.

It is vitally important that we do not constrain ourselves by any sense of determinism or moral cowardice that thwarts our better nature. We perpetually choose who we are, whether we recognize it or not. Sartre knew that existentialism's emphasis on personal freedom, as the natural vehicle for reason and compassion, provides a natural bulwark against all forms of totalitarianism, be it communism, fascism – or its more subtle and invasive form, consumerism.

Simply put, *freedom that is actualized* prevents the soulless conformity that totalitarianism needs to thrive. When freedom is based on activated conscience, Natural Law precludes the kind of radical behavior that results in despotism or hedonism. It joins freedom and morality together as inseparable.

Remember, existentialism tells us that we become who we *plan* to be – who we put effort into becoming. *(1ˢᵗ Trust: I will develop my life for the greater good.)* Anything less surrenders to absurdity.

## Chapter 11

# Kairos — *The Right Time*

The word *kairos* comes from Greek philosophy and can be roughly translated as *the right time*. It refers to a transformative event that changes the course of moral or intellectual history. Some Christian theologians, notably Paul Tillich, have described it as an auspicious point in time when history and eternity intersect to produce a spiritual turning point.

For our purposes, Kairos is recognized as a convergence of various factors that initiate dramatic change in consciousness. It starts when factors that are favorable to this change work their influence upon the way people think about themselves and the world they live in. At some point, this causes a significant leap in our cultural or spiritual evolution. Due to the complicated nature of a Kairos event, it cannot be predicted beforehand exactly what that change will be.

We recognize certain Kairos events taking place in the past.

The *Golden Age* of Classical Greece was one. History bears witness to a sudden burst of intellectual advancements that were drawn from few precedents. This led to astounding advancements in philosophy, art, theater, poetry, architecture, and the use of reason for basic scientific inquiry. Socrates, Plato, Aristotle, Hypocrites, Epicurus, Homer, Sophocles, Aeschylus, are just a few of the luminaries of this period that are astoundingly relevant even today.

The Golden Age was only one of a number of global inspirations that occurred at roughly the same time. Non-Western luminaries included such figures as Confucius, Buddha, Lao Tzu and Moses. With so many influential events arising almost simultaneously in different cultures, historians refer to this major

Kairos as the *Axial Age*.

Closer to our time, and perhaps just as important, was the *Age of Reason*, also known as the *Age of Enlightenment*. Its intellectual and philosophical momentum produced such notables as Francis Bacon, Isaac Newton, John Locke, Adam Smith, Voltaire, Rousseau, Denis Diderot, Montesquieu, Copernicus, Galileo, David Hume, Immanuel Kant and many others. Their legacy strongly influenced the experimental founding of the United States, the success of which inspired many other nations as well.

Enlightenment ideals stressed the potential of human reason, individual rights that were rooted in Nature's Law, free-market capitalism, popular literacy, a rejection of superstition and religious persecution, and a strong belief in the scientific method. Even the movements of the stars gradually surrendered their secrets to these disciplined, inquiring minds.

The Golden Age and the Age of Reason are considered the two major Kairos events of Western Civilization. Although there were other, less dramatic events as well, we can learn much by comparing the similarities of these two:

- Both events focused on freedom, individuality and human rights.
- Both utilized the clarity of reason to advance the human condition.
- Both questioned tradition and false beliefs while offering new insights.
- Both encouraged the intellectual capacities of people and fought against ignorance.
- Both experimented with liberal governments, including republics and democracies.
- Both strongly contributed to the idea of science improving the lives of others.

The Clasical Age was cut short because of a lack of unity among the Greek states, who had to defend themselves not only from outside invaders but from each other.

The Age of Reason subsided more quietly as the very advancements it produced led to smug complacency.

Although we still enjoy the many benefits from both of these Kairos events, what we have lost is their sense of intellectual integrity and inspiration.

Technological advancement is not enough. It never was. Authenticity is a matter of consciousness, of how genuinely we live our lives. Francis Bacon may have shown us how the scientific method succeeds by process alone, but that reflects nothing of the moral success or happiness of those who partake in or benefit from it.

Cell phones, computers and expensive miracle cures are false measurements of our success as moral creatures. We should measure instead the fulfillment of our ideals, our compassion for one another, including how we treat the least among us. Are people happy? Or are they just distracted from their inner pain? Is rampant escapism necessary? Are intoxicants still popular? Do we need more prisons? Or is civilization so improving that we can start tearing some of them down?

How many hours in a day do we sacrifice to mindless entertainment? What are we trying to avoid by doing so? People? Guilt? Dissatisfaction? Are we just trying to distract ourselves in order to avoid facing the absurdity of life?

The truth is that we cannot commercialize human nature and expect it to thrive. By becoming audiences instead of players, we are losing those qualities long deemed to be heroic. Instead, we live vicariously through an entertainment industry that does not have our best interests in mind.

In this way, we drift farther from our own potential.

* * *

**Understanding the implications of Kairos** helps us to see things from a different perspective.

How? By opening our eyes to the perceived direction of our own evolution. Kairos reminds us that we can contribute to and participate in something greater than ourselves. We are called to do so by our own instincts and moral inclinations.

Kairos events demonstrate that human evolution is sometimes propelled by incredible leaps of spiritual transformation.

Prior to each epoch, the elements of change gather and swell with new potential, which then waits for the right moment to happen. No matter what point in time that we find ourselves, we can contribute to that buildup by the ideals that we embrace and propagate. This is where we find purpose and meaning of the highest caliber that we might not have considered before.

We live in a world of motion, a world of interconnected, symbiotic factions where participants evolve and interrelate at the same time. By preserving our ideals, by living them in our daily lives, we assure that virtue, intelligence and thoughtful compassion continue their role in the evolution of our species.

Our choices, of course, remain our own. One might think that the possibility of destroying the world we live in would make us choose more carefully. Over and over our willing blindness proves that it is not. Pollution continues at unprecedented rates despite sharp increases of cancer, respiratory ailments and the frightful progression of climate change. War, genocide, terrorism, starvation, and even the threat of nuclear obliteration still continue. Some people go to great lengths to keep it that way – for no other reason than fear of change. In the wake of all this, the values we extol from history, tradition and religion become ever more shallow. As long as our personal needs are met, our egos sufficiently stroked and the media distracts us from our discontent, most of us care little about anything else.

What we need to remember is that whatever change awaits us

is at least partially of our own making. Each individual is part of a family that is part of a community or clan, that is part of a region and culture, that is part of a nation, that owes its very existence to the world of nature.

Accepting responsibility is the first step.

Making a positive commitment distinguishes today's knight from everyone else.

\* \* \*

**One cannot approach Kairos directly**. When we try to predict its coming, we are overwhelmed by complexities. Too many factors are at play. Everything that exists contributes to some extent. Potential detours are countless.

I sometimes compare that complexity to the semi-melodic chaos of musical instruments being tested before a play or concert begins. One cannot appreciate the orchestrated master-piece that follows by the disjointed bedlam that precedes it. Each instrument contributes bits and pieces to what is scarcely a hint of the same melody. At some point, however, the maestro taps his wand and everything comes together with formulated precision, all parts contributing to a single, beautiful whole.

Likewise, a Kairos event results from a sudden, transforma-tional combination of its disparate parts, each contributing toward a single development.

Francis Bacon, one of the original Enlightenment thinkers, was not born into a world that welcomed his innovative ideas. Schools were deeply invested in a status quo that limited their teaching to *Aristotelian Scholasticism*. Nevertheless, the readiness to change had long been stirring in the background. Bacon's critique brought an enthusiastic response – not so much by teachers as by the intellectuals that it liberated. Free thought and inquiry won the day, and a new age began.

If the preparations for change had not been made, however

subconsciously, people would not have responded as they did.

When a Kairos event happens, it takes whatever shape it will as various pieces unite to create something new.

Many of us today are so involved with our personal pursuits that we often fail to see the dynamics of change taking place. Each day seems much like the one before it. This is not surprising. The arrival of the Renaissance was hardly noticed by the majority of European peasants. Nevertheless, a new age had begun.

Some people prefer holding on to what they find familiar. They fail to see that the past that they mean to protect is what provided the necessity for change and provoked it to happen. Their resistance builds roadblocks to the natural course that the past has laid out for us, disrupting a smooth, positive transition. Likewise, trying to force change to happen when people are not ready inhibits what should come naturally. We cannot know precisely where change will lead, or what factors are necessary to make it work.

\* \* \*

**It is impossible to predict** where a Kairos event will lead, even for those in the midst of one, who consciously want to partake in its formation. Nevertheless, certain measures can help prepare them.

The first is recognizing that *nothing handicaps our observations more than pre-formed expectations*. We must not judge what is happening by our own preferences or personal agendas. Even if it seems that we are exactly on target, the process could change direction any moment.

The second is *opening our awareness* to the pulse of Nature's Law, which we experience through conscience and reason. Chivalry-Now assists by providing a simple code that balances the freedom and commitment that Nature's Law demands.

Third, it helps to *approach the possibility of Kairos with humility, respect, flexibility, intelligence – and a certain amount of awe.*

Fourth, we need to understand that *closed political ideologies are so contrived and morally questionable that they form a barrier to truth.* If you take on the rigid values of a liberal, conservative, libertarian, socialist or whatever, you end up seeing the world through the distortions of that particular lens, which makes it impossible to see a creative, unfettered Kairos for what it is. Truth does not mold itself according to authoritarian viewpoints, and that especially includes partisan ideologies.

For example, it is ludicrous to judge a nation solely by the size of its government or tax rate. Such criteria say nothing about justice, fairness, opportunity, or concern for human rights, no matter how they try to sell it. Small governments can be just as blood-thirsty as their larger, totalitarian cousins. Large governments can be so cumbersome and corrupt that the good of the people can be lost in bureaucracy. Better to judge a nation from a wider perspective, such as how it sees to the welfare of its people, or treats other nations.

\* \* \*

**Before our best intentions** run amok, it is important to understand that no one is wise enough to purposely orchestrate change on behalf of Kairos.

No one has the intelligence, foresight or moral authority to control or direct the burgeoning transformation of consciousness that Kairos brings about. Each epoch unfolds as it will because of the complexity of seemingly unrelated factors, including the readiness of people for change. Predictions are nothing more than guesswork, and should be treated as such. People certainly have influence, but no one is in control.

There is, however, an important role that each of us can play, no matter how distant or close the next Kairos event might be.

When we are true to our ideals in our everyday lives, we

preserve, strengthen and contribute those ideals to the world we live in. We add them to the equation.

This is the responsibility of all. The fate of Kairos is in our hands.

\* \* \*

**It is only natural to** hope that a Kairos event is imminent during our lifetimes.

Every generation feels that it lives at a special point in time. In certain respects they are. The world we live in is always changing. We repeatedly confront choices that ultimately shape the future. Even when we resist the current of change, it happens anyway. Far better to respond with enthusiasm and intelligence, and contribute the very best that human nature has to offer.

It is easy to feel small and insignificant in the light of huge cultural transformations. Nevertheless, just as in ages past, individuals form the bedrock of what follows.

During the founding of the United States, a unique association of individuals made the new republic possible. Washington, Adams, Jefferson, Madison, Franklin and others are still held in high esteem despite their faults, frailties and conflicts. As children of the Enlightenment, they contributed to a new vision of freedom that inspired not only a nation but the future of many nations.

This did not occur in a vacuum. Across the sea, ideas were being expounded that inspired their colonial aspirations. John Locke, Baron de Montesquieu and a hundred others paved the way by developing revolutionary ideas about civilian governments, equality, and human rights.

Nevertheless, what would have happened without the personal integrity of George Washington? The doggedly vain resolve of John Adams? The somewhat conflicted idealism of Thomas Jefferson? The good-natured pragmatism of Ben

Franklin? And James Madison's unpretentious ability to influence and inspire?

Their accomplishments reflected an idealism that probably would not have happened twenty years earlier or twenty years later. They certainly would not happen in our present political climate, where divisiveness is seen as the surest route toward power. Circumstances favorable to freedom and democracy propitiously converged in 1776 because the time was ripe for it to happen.

We might wonder if people were aware of the uniqueness of their times and what was happening.

They very much were, as evidenced by the words of George Washington in his *Circular Letter of 1783* (his last letter to the state governments as commander-in-chief). He may not have heard of Kairos, yet his words describe it very well.

"The foundation of our Empire was not laid in the gloomy age of Ignorance and Superstition, but at an Epocha when the rights of mankind were better understood and more clearly defined, than at any former period, the researches of the human mind, after social happiness, have been carried to a great extent, the Treasures of knowledge, acquired by the labors of Philosophers, Sages and Legislatures, through a long succession of years, are laid open for our use, and their collected wisdom may be happily applied in the Establishment of our forms of Government; the free culti-vation of Letters, the unbounded extension of Commerce, the progressive refinement of Manners, the growing liberality of sentiment, and above all, the pure and benign light of Revelation, have had ameliorating influence on mankind and increased the blessings of Society. At this auspicious period, the United States came into existence as a Nation, and if their Citizens should not be completely free and happy, the fault will be entirely their own."

I find the last sentence particularly significant in light of today's rabid discontent.

There are other examples of Kairos as well.

Mohandas Gandhi's liberation movement in India succeeded not only because of his efforts, but because of the time and circumstances in which it occurred. Ethnocentric imperialism was already being questioned by the conscience of the English people, many of whom wished the Mahatma well.

Martin Luther King's fight for equal rights resonated because many people of all colors were appalled by the unfairness and hypocrisy of segregation.

In each of these events, leaders spoke to the ready conscience of sympathetic people, most of whom were eager to respond.

The Nativity stories of Christianity describe a waiting anticipation for the Messiah's coming. This included shepherds, wise men, kings and people at large who felt oppressed by Roman rule. All these factors, including Rome's oppression, contributed to the building of what theologians determined to be a Kairos event. The times were ready, expectations were high, and a new threshold of spiritual consciousness was born. Not everyone changed, of course, and not right away. Kairos events are never all-inclusive. Nevertheless, something happened that could not be stopped. A seed was planted that would produce a new way of life.

As participants in our own culture, we play a role in actualizing whatever change awaits us. We contribute to it positively or negatively in everything we do or fail to do. We either strengthen or weaken it; facilitate or delay it; contribute to or detract from it; increase its energy, or dilute it with narcissistic disinterest.

As modern knights, we are called upon to preserve our ideals in the way we live. Doing so, we hope to inspire others to see their lives in a quest-like fashion as well.

We can draw freely from what we have learned from the concepts of Esoterica, and our experiences of all life.

We can open our hearts and minds to the direct teachings of *Nature's Law;* we can make a strong commitment to the virtue and reason of *Areté;* we can enter into a respectful partnership with nature based on *Ordo Mundi;* we can dedicate ourselves to the fullness of truth as accessed by *Aletheia;* we can fulfill the inner direction of our lives through *Telos;* the use of *reason* and *responsibility* ties it all together.

These concepts came to us through an unbroken chain of cultural insights dating back thousands of years. If we learn from their wisdom and apply them responsibly, we become soldiers of Kairos in everything we do.

\* \* \*

**No matter** where the quest leads us, no matter how insane the world seems, no matter how deeply we find ourselves in the dregs of despair, we have one strong hope to look forward to. *Kairos events happen.* The human spirit still manages to crop up now and then and push us forward.

To actually experience one, to see its beneficence ripple out with new vision and expectations, is to be transformed by incredible passion and excitement, as evidenced by those whose writings come down to us from the past. One might call it an awakening, a social *anagnorisis* – after which nothing is ever the same.

There is another side to consider, however.

History shows us that the initial wave of *Kairos* transformation, potent as it is, is followed by a receding tide.

As change settles, its unique inspiration gradually loses its power and seeps back into the landscape. The tide seeps away and only the shore remains, somewhat different than before, revealing new treasures for those who look among the scars and debris. Eventually it becomes familiar and forms its own uninspired status quo.

The cycle of progress and regression seems unavoidable. Something is gained, whole, pristine and shining – and then recedes into convention. Consider how the ancient philosophies eventually fell to barbarism, and Christianity splintered into competing sects. Even chivalry lost much of its solid warrior ethic. As it became more courtly, it became effete as well. To many today, chivalry means little more than the quaint custom of opening doors for ladies.

At the onset, the bright promise of America's ideals did not extend itself to slaves and indigenous people. Even women and non-land-owning white males were refused suffrage. Gandhi's crowning achievement, a free and united India, eventually divided into separate nations that continue to threaten each other even today. The soul of the Enlightenment was eventually replaced by the rapaciousness of consumerism and partisanship.

Humanity progressed despite all this. Two steps forward, one step back, still makes for progress. Lessons are learned that eventually make way for something else.

Sensibilities change. They evolve – hopefully for the better, but not always. When change happens, people have to decide how to respond. One can only wonder what would have happened if people were only more aware.

This awareness is where we need to concentrate our attention. If virtue is preserved and strong in a given culture, it stands to reason that it will play a decisive role in shaping what comes next. If it is lax, if greed and selfishness dominate, opportunities are lost and ultimate goals delayed.

Existentialism tells us that each person is responsible for defining humanity. Kairos illustrates how true that is. As a species, we are the accumulation of what is best and worst in all of us. It is important to always choose the best.

Look around. If a Kairos were to happen today, how would we greet it? With anger? Paranoia? With long-entrenched greed? Apathy? Would we be too busy rushing to exploit our neighbor to even notice? Or wasting time with sitcoms or video games? Would we allow the tunnel vision of political ideologies to ruin its direction?

Or would we greet it with open minds and hearts, receptive to possibilities?

\* \* \*

**Like many who came before us**, we citizens of the West perceive ourselves as living in the best and worst of times. For every problem that gets solved by brilliant ingenuity, two others take its place.

We flaunt our pride and deftly hide our shame. The comforts we enjoy and have long taken for granted are suddenly found to be toxic. Our friends can do no wrong; our enemies do nothing right. We rejoice in the acquisition of hard-earned wealth, and then slide into decadence. We lecture the world about human rights, and then fail to uphold them ourselves. Celebrities glitter as the homeless starve. We expect the God who blesses the poor and condemns hypocrisy to support our prejudices. False prophets rise among us, repeatedly fall, and we still cling to them for guidance.

The best of times; the worst of times. Kairos has no respect for ideological extremism. It seeks to create something new.

The liberal thinks he can help this happen with a soft heart and good intentions. The conservative thinks he can stop it by saying no. The student of Kairos knows better. He takes his obligations seriously, working quietly and intently to protect virtue as best he can.

Simple logic cuts through all the banter and contention:

- We cannot long enjoy the benefits of national wealth if it is based on runaway deficits.
- We cannot grow our economy to the point of saving us

from pollution, war and a clash of ideologies. The wealthier we become, the more we pollute and assert our will over others, even when it is contrary to our own principles.

- We cannot trust politicians who are indebted to powerful special interests. This is where corruption begins.
- Economic regulations may help to protect the environment and national economy, but they fail to solve the underlying problem, which is greed.
- We cannot kill all the people in the world whom we consider a threat.

It seems obvious that failed solutions only make things worse, yet we employ them anyway as if we cannot break the habit. This produces a dysfunctional relationship between rational thought and virtue on one side, and stubborn, childish demands on the other. We cannot blame this entirely on ignorance. Greed and apathy are just as culpable.

Always remember: *There is no hypocrisy of little consequence when its pervasiveness makes hypocrites of us all.*

This is not child's play. Hard choices have to be made if we want to be true advocates of our ideals.

- We have no right to assert our will over peaceful nations, or let our businesses exploit them.
- We can no longer ignore those suffering from poverty or rampant disease as if they somehow deserve their fate.
- If we cannot eradicate prejudice, then we must at least resist our own biases while protecting the rights of others as a matter of principle.
- Sacrificing the planet that we all depend on to greed-generated pollution is not a viable option.
- More bombs is not the answer.
- More casinos and celebrities merely divert us from what

needs to be done.

- No amount of complaining or money or new technology can save us from ourselves.

Most social problems spring from our own shortcomings. Only by recognizing this can we properly begin to fix them. In our laziness, apathy and partisan fervor, we might prefer something simpler, like a miracle cure or messianic event. Unfortunately, hoping or complaining do nothing but delay a serious response.

While we might welcome a Kairos event to turn that all around, it is difficult to see one coming. Everything seems to point in the opposite direction. Democracy is failing for want of honesty and intelligent citizen involvement. The steady stream of technological conveniences leaves little time for reflection and distracts us from issues of importance. War has migrated and mutated into a stream of terrorism that threatens the future of civilization. Nature is something we ignore, exploit and desperately try to rescue – all at the same time. No longer does it serve us as something to learn from and hold in reverence. The earth responds to our selfishness with climate change and all kinds of natural disaster.

The future of humanity looks grim.

Is there any hope on the horizon? Will an avalanche of negative consequences provoke us to set things right? Or is it too late already?

If a Kairos event is fomenting, it must be radically different from anything our limited understanding might expect.

We see a lot of anger and frustration, but little effort toward positive change. Mostly we hear complaints or stubborn denial. No movement toward reason and compassion seems to be brewing. No heroes are cropping up that we can truly admire. Just a lot of posturing among those in power who would exploit any tragedy for personal gain.

We cannot know what form the next Kairos event will take.

Will a quiet rebirth of human sanity spread across the globe of its own accord? Will well-reasoned, good intention rule the day?

Or will we suffer for our sins in a cataclysm of our own making?

\* \* \*

**Today's values are such** that we are taught to judge ourselves, our actions and our values materialistically. The big house. The fancy car. Bloated bank accounts and diversified portfolios. More possessions.

None of these things are wrong in themselves. What is troubling is how they draw our attention away from what really matters. When we constantly measure our lives according to the acquisition of *things*, our thoughts and values become misplaced. Life cannot be measured by materialism. The only valid measurement is who we are as people. We must look to Areté, the *highest virtue*, for that.

Contributing to an environment of greed, ignoring responsibilities to others, encouraging vice, spreading falsehood, catering to ego instead of conscience, not only detracts from the authenticity of who we are, it turns us into small and petty creatures. It prevents us from finding the autonomy that comes from completeness. Autonomy does not attach itself to possessions or false values without losing its own value.

Accumulation of wealth says nothing of personal goodness. Like power, it can be more of a liability than an asset. A man without virtue and respect for truth is inherently stymied and incomplete.

The lesson to be learned from the possibility of Kairos is one of overarching purpose. Lived properly, our lives add purpose and meaning to the world. We have strong reason not only to be good, but to excel, to aid those who are in need, to stand up for justice, to see truth as only humility can unveil it, and help others do the same.

With all this in mind, Kairos consideration has the power to unite us in the present for the sake of the future.

\* \* \*

**One of the lessons to be drawn** from Kairos is the interrelationship of all things. We are not disconnected from the complexity of life around us. We may perceive ourselves as separate, with varying degrees of success, but that neither prevents change, nor stops us from being affected. What it does is make us either irrelevant or an outright enemy of life.

For all we know, whatever change awaits us may be programmed in our genes. That would certainly explain the Axial Ages of antiquity and the 17th century, where inspiration seemed endemic and eventually became globally profound.

We are all in this together. Either we ride the wave of change or we drown in it. For this reason, we should concern ourselves with what is happening in the world. We are responsible for the preservation of our ideals, whether a Kairos event is imminent or not.

No doubt there were people who thought that Socrates was just an eccentric crank, an annoying gadfly best to ignore. Neighboring city-states might not have even heard of him at the time. They had no idea of the future impact of this one man's constant questioning – a man, it is well noted, who died prematurely and never bothered to preserve his own ideas for posterity.

Should we be looking for a charismatic leader like Socrates to arise and open the door to human fulfillment? If we do, we will probably empower some charlatan instead, who will push us back into another age of darkness. The only integrity we can be sure of is our own, and only then when we guard it dearly. We must beware of the political sound bites that play upon our anger and irrational fears. They steer us away from thinking for ourselves.

Kairos makes a strong argument that our lives, our values, our actions and beliefs contribute to shaping the future. How could they not?

The more we surrender to illusions, the stronger they become, allowing our grasp of what is real and meaningful to slip away.

A strong regard for truth and virtue helps sustain truth and virtue in the world. That is the responsibility Areté brings, and each of us is required to do our part. No one will heal our culture for us.

Keep in mind, Kairos does not pick and choose. It works with what it has. Feed it denial, selfishness and greed, and we cripple it, perhaps for centuries to come. This might explain the lengthy and sometimes regressive gaps between one Kairos event and another.

Feed it justice, courtesy and love, and a solid foundation is laid. We become champions for truth when we bring virtue to the table and open people's eyes to deceit.

From this perspective, a new form of knighthood presents itself for consideration – one that commits itself to facilitating Kairos' intricate weave.

The protector of Kairos looks upon culture and society as things that are constantly in flux, progressing one moment, regressing the next, sometimes doing both at the same time. Something new arises, while something else is lost. Ideologies clash and transform at the same time. Ideas mix and contribute to the process. Preferences change. It is difficult to evaluate anything for its permanence.

When we see this clearly, our instincts call us to preserve the values that contribute to the right direction. We know that certain values are always beneficial, such as truth, justice, mercy, and defense of the innocent. We are called to keep those values alive for posterity, anticipating change with new hope for the future.

In a sense, we become keepers of the Holy Grail.

# Chapter 12

# Kairos—*Part 2*

**We have explained the word Kairos** as meaning *the right time* or *readiness*, a particular moment when various forces converge and produce major transformations in human consciousness, be it social, cultural, spiritual, or all three.

There is another meaning to consider as well.

When we use *kairos* with a small "k," it refers to the present moment, with all its possibilities and potential. Each moment is the culmination of all that has come before it. The convergence of contributing factors that go into it provide us with the opportunity for insight, action and personal growth. This ever-present kairos asserts the unique importance of every moment in everything we do – every event and discussion, word and whisper, the direction and momentum of every thought. To be aware of this kairos is to attend to the moment fully, to see opportunities one might otherwise miss, and to express our values and ideals in the here and now. Awareness of the kairos moment makes possible the breaking forth or actualization of personal authenticity in the here and now.

The larger concept of Kairos reflects the relationship of significant events, mores, and creative responses that make widespread change inevitable.

The smaller, ever-present *kairos*, scarcely noticed and usually uneventful, calls for a sharpened awareness of life within the flow of time. The larger version depends on it.

Major Kairos events have been metaphorically described as a particular intersection (or collision) of time <u>with</u> eternity that produces an indelible mark, a breakthrough or major turning point in our consciousness.

Little kairos is what theologian Paul Tillich called the "God-given moment," the intersection of time _and_ eternity, spirit and matter, that makes awareness and potentiality possible.

(Please note: To be applicable to the widest audience possible, I use the word _spirit_ to mean the combination of consciousness, intellect, emotion, intuition and memory that comprises the human mind and much of our deepest experience. Spirit can be described as the _indefinable sum_ of consciousness that produces something unique from its contributory parts. I therefore purposely avoid reference to some incorporeal life or energy that exists beyond the realm of matter.)

The message of kairos in the temporal sense is this: when we move through time unaware of its possibilities, ignoring its many opportunities, locked in a repetitive mindset that never varies, shaped by prejudice, and numb to the flow of life of which we are part, we squander our existence. We lose awareness of our own vital presence within the living moment. We see the world not directly, but through a fog of memory, through what is stale and self-contained in our minds. Instead of sailing on the immediate passage of time, we find ourselves caught in its wake, more in touch with the past than with the moment's actualization.

Today's knighthood draws us back into a direct experience of this on-going kairos, the living moment. When we commit ourselves to the quest, we open our lives to awareness and authenticity, where the virtues of the greatest good, Areté, stand clear in their priority and development. This, in itself, awakens us to the here and now, maximizing our experience of the kairos moment.

I believe that when we commit ourselves to expanding human consciousness on a global scale, the functions of kairos join with those of greater Kairos as one.

Even so, the future cannot be known. All we really know is that each moment that we live, every choice that we make, contributes to its final outcome. That should be enough to motivate us to always do what is right.

## Chapter 13

# Mystic Realities — *Grail Consciousness and More*

**We live in an age of unprecedented** knowledge, comfort and convenience. Technology advances so quickly that few can keep up with it. We anticipate the next innovations with an impatience that makes it difficult to appreciate what we have.

Despite all our possessions and achievements, however, we remain discontent, needing constant distractions just to maintain a functional level of energy. Hence the need for hundreds of cable channels that seem to provide something for every taste but our own.

Instead of walking tall and proud and appreciatively aware of our surroundings, as nobility would have it, our heads are bowed while texting someone equally as bored with the lifestyle that consumerism brought us. Or we whittle away our time speaking into cell phones about nothing. Computer games create alternative realities that are more exciting than the real thing, with the added benefit of no actual risk. So-called *reality* television convinces us that fake lives captured on camera are somehow more real and important than our own. We are invited to experience them vicariously instead of building the excitement of our own lives, and sadly many of us do.

Whereas technology once provided tools for better living, we are now becoming appendages to machines that determine how we spend our time and how we think of the world.

What rewards do we get in return? Unending entertainment and accumulated junk – the kind of addictive distraction that promises to make life without purpose a little more bearable, even as it robs us of the natural cure – our own humanity.

What will the continuation of these mind-numbing distractions do in a few short decades? What will we become? What new addictions will we need to carry us through the day once the old ones lose their luster? Will our only encounter with silence and self-reflection come from the occasional inconvenience of a power outage?

Today's intrusive technology is replacing our awareness of the here and now. It distracts us from the very real Mystery of life, which is the foundation upon which we stand. We call this Mystery spiritual, and have reverenced it since humanity first contemplated its own existence. For millennia we have identified ourselves with some form of spiritual/mystical awareness and, at some level in our nature, this process has served us well.

The magic of technology is pulling us away from this fundamental awareness, forcing our spiritual potential to atrophy. The lure and addiction is so profound that it draws many of us away from nature as if nature has nothing to offer, and might actually be our enemy.

I am reminded of the impact of the Industrial Revolution – how millions of lives were transformed overnight, tearing people away from the rural living that they were used to, herding them into unsanitary cities, where pollution and cultural degradation were inevitable. Men who once partnered with nature were now confined to assembly-line monotony, enriching the lives of business owners far more than their own. Families had to adjust to the absence of their fathers and husbands.

No one could predict the outcome of what was being lost, not the least of which were consistent relationships between father and child, husband and wife. Eventually, mothers had to enter the workforce as well. Family dynamics had to be redefined – and not necessarily for the better.

We are undergoing similar changes today without considering where they will lead.

My critique is not meant to discourage change – far from it. I think that change is desperately needed. My concern is that we face terrible risks when we respond to major change with blinders on, and our future is decided by the amorality of the marketplace. Certain cultural aspects need to be preserved, such as virtue and human dignity and dynamics that nurture our humanity, rather than detract from it. It helps to see where we are going.

That means approaching life *prospectively* in a way that preserves the values that we hold sacred. If we do not, there is no telling where the march of progress might lead. Perhaps to our own demise.

To avoid that, it is time to reclaim and preserve our inherent spirituality, and express it in ways that are appropriate to our future.

* * *

**Our journey begins** with experiencing the ever-present weave and flow of the *kairos* moment that cleaves the divide between past and future. Simple awareness of the here and now places us exactly where we are – which is always at the edge of Mystery.

Our perception of time, our predilections toward thinking of the past and worrying about the future, can be so powerful that they distract us from experiencing the moment at hand. This results in a diversion of consciousness from what is real to what does not exist except as memories or projections.

That we exist in the present, that narrow line of engagement where the immediate future actualizes itself and then quickly disappears, is the most profound mystery of them all – a mystery not only of time, with its seemingly endless yet transitory nature, but of existence, and our ability to reflect on it.

We exist, rather than not. How is that possible?

Is there a reason or purpose for our existence?

Our rational minds like to think so. But what if there is no reason or purpose? Have we stumbled upon the rational mind's absurdity of all absurdities? Or can we find purpose and meaning by creating them ourselves, as existentialism insists? Perhaps our inner aim, our Telos, is exactly that – to bring profound purpose and meaning to the world of nature.

Whether we recognize it or not, our conscious minds live nowhere else but in the ever-changing moment. We are dependent upon this evasive, temporal flow into which we are born and from which we will someday leave. The only word I can think of to describe it is *miraculous*.

Should we participate in this miracle while running on automatic pilot? That would hardly be participating at all.

It is time to explore the Mystery of life in order to learn what significance we have, and what we should do because of it.

\* \* \*

**The Mystery of life reveals itself** as it will – sometimes in glimpses or lingering silence, sometimes in a sudden flash of insight, or a wordless whisper that is stunningly profound.

We respond as if called by a lost memory that yearns to be found. That is no coincidence. *Aletheia* equates truth with *finding* and *remembering*. When we surrender to this experience, confusion dissipates, if only for a moment, and is replaced by feelings of affirmation. And if that house of cards that we call ego collapses in its wake, we find ourselves suddenly free.

Legends of the quest carry with them the lure of spiritual awakening. As we progress, we find ourselves longing to see, touch and hear what only the heart can recognize – and even then only indirectly. We associate this psychological/spiritual process with the *Quest for the Holy Grail*.

The Grail represents the ineffable. No matter what its symbolism suggests, be it a cup or jewel or platter, it always points to something else, drawing us into a sense of mystery. We are reminded that the fullness of truth always surpasses our understanding. The most we can do is relate to it as best we can.

We find intimations of the Grail in art, poetry and music. It might be the siren's song caught on canvas, or a contemplative phrase sparking revelations far greater than the words themselves. We often find it in our confrontation with nature, when the mind opens up to a beautiful sunset or the stillness of twilight, or when sunlight sparkles on the intricate segments of a dragonfly's wing. We relax to the possibilities of cloud-shapes as they stir the imagination before changing their shapes and moving on. We grasp a particular moment with the hope of remembering its serene perfection. We recognize that it is telling us *something* – we know not what. Our instincts recognize manifestations of truth that our minds fail to comprehend. We become like children, accepting what is beyond our capacity to understand.

Deep in our hearts we know that our search for meaning carries existential imperatives. Not knowing where it leads, however, we fear the abyss that lies beyond. Can *silence* be heard? Can *nothingness* be tasted?

Meditative moments suggest that they can.

We search for songs that will guide us – hymns, love songs, rap, a marching beat, a joyful tune or bitter lament. We need to dance in celebration of the moment.

But the *deeper song*, that inner dirge, the very soul that weeps for liberation, we shy away from, or try shaping it to fit some artificial tune. The words are whispered by no one in particular, yet echo throughout our being, the constant pulse repeating its message: *Here I am. But why? What is the secret that lies right before me, that cannot be seen?*

The deeper song is life itself, seeking to understand – no whisper from the gods or muse; no sign from heaven or ancient script; no omen or shift of constellations. It is the urge that gives us life, that challenges the dull continuum by asking: *What now?*

*Surely there is more? I am incomplete without it.*

Sometimes, very quietly, we hear its whispered reply urging us on:

*Yes, indeed. There is always more.*

The deeper song sings of a rich nobility for us all that is yet unclaimed. It summons us to find and bring forth *whatever it is that moves us.* The answer to a question perhaps. A new remedy. The kind of hope that overcomes doubt. If not transcendence, then maybe, just maybe, a better, more meaningful moment *right now.*

The *12 Trusts* and Esoterica, the code and philosophical roots of Chivalry-Now, reflect evidence of that deeper song. They express who we are when we are at our best.

\* \* \*

**Although the spirituality** of Chivalry-Now permeates all its ideals, let us consider it for the moment as its own domain.

When I refer to the spirituality of Chivalry-Now, I am not referring to an invisible world of angels and demons, or an indescribable dimension somehow separate from time and space. I am not referencing anything outside of our everyday experience. This is, after all, the world we live in. We can realistically explore no other. What spirituality refers to is that there is more to our experience of the world than we normally recognize. Nothing could be more plain.

The spirit of Chivalry-Now is grounded in fact and available to anyone, no matter what their creed or lack thereof. It tells us that we do not need a profound leap of faith to discover our spiritual awareness. What we seek is always right in front of us.

Our definition of spirituality is simple and believable. It is a conscious relationship with the Mystery that we live in and are part of – *the Mystery of existence.* We refer to this as Mystery because we know that the universe exists but cannot explain how or from where it came to being. Time itself escapes our grasp of understanding. Does time pass? Or does it carry us forward along with it? The best we can do is measure it, and even that contradicts our experience of its flow. Consciousness shows that life consists of inexplicable properties.

We normally disregard such mysteries. They interfere with the tangibles of everyday living. This avoidance leads to spiritual numbness. When we base our values on the conviction that there is no fundamental Mystery, our minds effectively shut themselves off from what we do not know. We lose that sense of awe that accentuates our awareness.

It is probably true that we will never understand the cause of our existence, nor the fabric of our own consciousness for that matter. But do we have to? *By simply acknowledging our limits, we accept the Mystery for what it is, which is something unexplained.* Once we do that, our relationship with truth automatically becomes more complete.

We live in a world of contrasts and paradox.

\* \* \*

**On the side of** tradition, religions offer us their rich symbolism and depth of spiritual conjectures. They point to scriptures for their authority, scriptures based on faith.

On the other side, consumerism constantly entices us with the insistence that all we need to care about is sweetening our lives with trinkets of the marketplace.

Either way we are being told what to think and how to act, and are subtly cautioned not to ask too many questions. The inherent message, that we should rely on others for our explanation and experience of reality, not only inhibits our potential as rational human beings, it pulls us away from a direct relationship with the Mystery around us.

No matter how we are distracted or restrained, Mystery

remains what it is – silent, transparent, ever-present – and yet, in many ways, more real than the illusions that tug us in every direction. Everything we see, including us, would not exist except for the paradox of something coming from nothing. It is this indescribable magician's hat where our train of reason breaks down, and reflective appreciation begins.

Here we find the source of nothingness within which everything exists. Here we find the ubiquitous question mark that both precedes and answers all our questions without words.

We liken this awareness to the Holy Grail.

* * *

*Grail Consciousness is the mindset* that occurs when one awakens to the mystery of life and responds accordingly. It is the awareness sparked by the direct experience of living when our attention is not misdirected by illusions. Grail Consciousness is what makes Areté, the highest expression of human nature, possible in the deepest sense. The transformational event we call anagnorisis breaks through to a more complete awareness of the here and now.

Grail Consciousness produces a state of mind that makes our subjective relationship to truth, as Aletheia, possible. When we truly engage life as a quest, we experience not only its length and breadth, but also its depth, which includes our own innermost core, our moral conscience. This is where we find our connection with truth, producing the kind of direct participation in life that we describe as *authenticity*.

As the etymology of Aletheia reveals, it takes what is *hidden within us* and makes it experiential, *remembered*, or *no longer hidden*. This completes us. It makes us more human, more alive, which is Aletheia's *not-death* experience.

Chivalry-Now does not offer an escape from pain or withdrawal from the world of conflict of which we are part. It does not accept the doctrine that proclaims a universal "balance of good and evil." Neither does it aim to liberate one's mind from thought and desire, which would separate us from our own nature.

Quite the opposite. It seeks a bold, life-affirming immersion into reality that includes the finest aspects of our nature, no matter how imperfect, especially our passion for ideals and progress. It promotes *contemplative enhancement* rather than *meditative elimination;* productive striving rather than nonproductive stillness; engaging in life's struggles rather than avoiding or tolerating them through detachment.

Not all *desire* is evil, as some philosophies suggest. Grail Consciousness holds as sacred the desire for what is good – it desires to eliminate human pain and suffering as much as possible through the use of reason and compassion. It desires a better world for everyone.

Grail Consciousness does not recognize a measured harmony of *male and female energies* – whatever that could mean in the real world. It seeks the liberated cooperation between actual men and actual women founded on equality, love, genuine respect and mutual interest.

Grail Consciousness does not search for other dimensions of life that cannot be seen, heard, touched or sensed in any way. It concentrates on what is real instead. With an appreciative nod toward Mystery, it searches for truth directly and for wherever it leads.

Grail Consciousness has little to do with the still, empty mind of Eastern tranquility. It seeks a full, active and self-disciplined mind instead, dedicated to the immediacy of the quest.

Of course we value stillness and silence when it attunes us to the creativity of the subconscious. Such a mind facilitates positive contemplation. This is not an *emptiness* of mind, but rather an *openness*, a receptivity, a listening to one's inner workings for the insight that it brings.

Our activated moral centers complete who we are to make Grail Consciousness possible. They tell us that freedom is synonymous with responsibility, and that moral commitment either expresses itself in action, or is false.

Enlightenment for the West does not aim at some sort of transcendence into another realm of being. It seeks to actively engage truth within reality itself. Aletheia shows us that truth is part of us already, something to reclaim, remember, and make unhidden – in order to experience life in its abundance.

This heightened consciousness is so real, so immediately accessible, that some might wonder if it is not transcendent enough.

They may feel skeptical about an approach that embraces so much of what Eastern mysticism pulls away from. While we might share with the East a love for simplicity, it does not hamper our drive for progress and innovation. We must then, of course, be held accountable for what we do, and resist the misuse of power that progress makes possible. The innocence we seek as our priority is not that of passivity, ignorance or naïveté. *It is the innocence of not being guilty.*

With that priority in mind, Chivalry-Now calls for the maturity of purpose that freedom demands. Its greatest enemies are the trappings of greed and the dullness of mind that comes from lack of use.

Those seeking nirvana or escape from the world of pain should look elsewhere. Our tangible goal, beyond the cultivation of virtue in our lives, is the building of a better world.

The quest teaches us that the true Mystery of life is so subtle and so sublime, that we need not include religious dogma in this philosophy, despite their obvious relationship. Matters of faith belong to each individual as part of his or her quest. We respect that. Matters of virtue, however, belong to us all. They form common ground for all of us, and can serve as a focal point for unity.

The quest remains unique for everyone. We each travel a path intrinsic to who we are. No path is better or worse than the other, as long as we learn from it as we should. Comparisons are difficult. When it comes to personal growth, it is possible for a life of want and suffering to produce greater results than a life of privilege. I have seen this first hand.

Each choice that confronts us can strengthen our moral resolve. The way we respond fashions our nobility or lack thereof. Life has no substitute. Either we live it with full integrity, or tragically fall short.

The Western path is not easy. We have no gurus, and there are no simple formulas for success, especially today. We live in a messy world that surrounds us with conflicting values and constant distractions. To make matters worse, each of us entertains personal dragons of our own, be they fears or prejudices, inherited ideologies, peer pressure, or the remnants of childhood pain or trauma. Ego obsession can be the most destructive dragon of all.

There is no escape from the reality we live in. But then, why should we want to escape it? Replacing reality with illusions or other kinds of escapism is an affront to truth – which is an affront to Areté. The quest encourages us to embrace what we see, and change things for the better.

The most important aspect of the quest is the journey itself, with its edifying challenges. We need no final goal, no loss of self into a greater Self, no escape from a continual cycle of rebirth. Whether we believe in God or not, our shared focus on ideals gives depth to everything we believe in.

The quest pushes us to live life in full consciousness and in defense of what is right. When we achieve authenticity, we contribute something of great value, not only to the present, but to the spiritual evolution of our species.

The strict evolutionist might question that statement. Evolution, after all, is decided by natural selection alone. It does not recognize the inclusion of *purpose*.

While in theory that is true, the introduction of human thought, compassion and technology dramatically changes the equation. We have the power to influence our own evolution. We can, to a limited but important extent, change things when we want to. Consciousness, reason and ingenuity give us the ability to direct our own growth. Survival of the fittest is being challenged everyday. Through purposeful effort, the weak and the infirm survive far better than they did even fifty years ago. Thanks to medical breakthroughs and social safety-nets, many people enjoy a longevity who otherwise might not.

The truth is that we constantly shape our evolution to no small degree. Things are not as haphazard as before. Education, applied intelligence, respect for law, generosity, forgiveness and courtesy steer us away from the law of the jungle. Natural disasters are met with quick, urgent responses that were not possible in the distant past.

Our obligation to all this boils down to the need for knowledgeable, purposeful self-development and a commitment to honorable choices.

And if, in the end, we learn that a mindless universe has no particular purpose for creatures of thought and moral integrity, all is not lost. We are still capable of shaping our own purpose and reaping benefits for everyone. To that end, it is imperative to build and preserve a moral foundation for which our progeny will be proud.

While there is nothing magical or mystical about any of this, it is here that we find what might be called the *mystical attraction* to chivalry. It is a focus of consciousness that can serve as a moral force in the world. It philosophically and metaphysically unites all that is good in us. Here we find purpose and meaning that are real.

Those who hold chivalry dear understand how achieving a moral life launches new levels of personal attainment. Truth calls us to reject the ways of falsehood and hidden agendas. The honorable simplicity of chivalry's code resonates in our hearts with certitude.

While we may view this as a significant shift in consciousness, it is nothing more than the full experience of being who we really are.

### Steps for achieving Grail Consciousness:

- Find your moral center. The *12 Trusts* can help you with that.
- Integrate your moral center into everyday life in order to complete who you are. Areté includes both reason and compassion.
- Live a life of integrity and purpose that reflects this authenticity.
- Search for what is true at every moment, so you aren't misguided by what is false.

Grail Consciousness is the well-meaning attentiveness of your completed self.

\* \* \*

**A moral code that** fails to appreciate and contribute to the inner workings of the soul is just another set of rules, no matter how liberal or conservative – another form of bondage instead of autonomy. Liberation of the mind comes about only when we *give consciousness its due*. The purpose of the quest is this very liberation.

The legendary Quest for the Holy Grail informs us that we are incomplete without our moral centers. Conscience is part of who we are. It is where personal virtue is derived. In order for us to be complete, we need it to be active in our daily lives. Virtue comes to life when reason directs it properly. This is the challenge that life lays before us, the challenge not just *to be*, but *to become* – to help, to share, to rescue, to love completely.

In other words, *to fully live!*

It is not enough for thinking persons just to mature into physical adulthood, get a job and raise a family. We need to incorporate meaning into our lives. Spiritual growth is as vital to our nature as physical growth.

Unfortunately, its attainment is not automatic, and comes with no guarantee.

\* \* \*

**Grail Consciousness is the immediate** experience of life that blossoms from a reverence for truth. Here we find the seriousness, inspiration and drive that excites the mind to authentic living. It is here that consciousness extends to peak awareness, experiencing the moment in pure, unadulterated living. Here we poetically touch what is eternal in each moment's extenuating fragment – *here in this moment*, and in *this* as well, and in each one passing. It is only here where clarity and vision become real, allowing us to speak for the greater good, imperfect though we are.

Because the Western path is synonymous with a life lived fully, it is wrought with the perils, distractions and propensity for error that life naturally brings. There is no escape from these challenges, which give life its quest-like quality. What Grail Consciousness provides is the means toward a goal that we all recognize as unreachable, yet still worthy of our greatest efforts. Here we find the stimulus to be who we really are – imperfect, fully human, yet essentially good – hopefully getting better. One might consider this the next phase of our evolution.

\* \* \*

**Medieval tales about the Holy Grail** offer insights into our relationship with the Mystery we live in. They reflect archetypal lessons that are imbedded in our Western psyche. Through symbols provided by myth and legend, they offer insights collected over millennia. Symbols often express what words cannot. These confrontations between human consciousness and Mystery still resonate with meaning.

The Grail stories tell about a knightly quest for an object called *the Grail*. It is usually described as a chalice or platter, but also a stone. Some describe it as the cup of the Last Supper, but its roots are far more ancient.

The story's protagonist is usually a knight of youthful inexperience. One day, he enters a mysterious castle where the Grail King lives. The Grail King is crippled, suffering from an old wound that never healed. Just before they dine, the knight is presented with a vision of the Grail (which represents the mysterious providence of life). The object generates light that fills the hall and is venerated by the castle residents. The young knight sees this, but fails to ask what it is.

This failure to inquire about the mystery before him proves to be a terrible mistake. In the presence of Mystery, he denied the nature of his own curiosity and desire for truth. Indeed, the castle inhabitants were waiting for him to ask about its meaning and significance, as if it were a rite-of-passage. He failed what the Grail demands of us all.

Consider how this differs from other mythical stories, where the hero is challenged by some threat, or confronted by a riddle he must answer. Instead, Mystery unveils itself for a moment, and he is expected to respond. When he does not, the opportunity passes. The castle and the Grail vanish from sight.

He later learns that if he had asked the right questions, the wounded Grail King would have been healed. In Celtic myth, the king represents both the land and the people on it. When the King suffers, so does everything else. The realm becomes a wasteland where people can barely survive. It was in the power of the young knight's expression of humanity to end that misery.

The well-meaning knight seeks to rectify his mistake. He searches for the Grail Castle, but cannot find it.

He confronts many adventures along the way, and learns lessons from them all. After months or even years of searching, he finally encounters the Grail Castle again, sees the Grail just as before, and inquires about its secret. The King is instantly healed and the land with him.

This young knight was a follower of a chivalric code meant to shape him as a force for good against injustice. But there is more to life than combating evil and slaying dragons. There is Mystery to confront, a profound Mystery that shows itself only sporadically and in unexplainable ways.

It is difficult to describe, but the experience is very real. Poetry provides our best expression, because in poetry words can launch themselves far beyond their otherwise limited meaning. We find glimpses of this in the bible as references to God:

*"I Am, That I Am,"* (or "I Am Who Am" RSV)
*"Be still, and know that I am God."*

We generally refer to these happenings as *mystical experiences,* but that misses the mark. It is a universal experience that occurs to us all at some point in our lives. Unfortunately, like the young knight, we usually fail to respond. Deciphering it as just a strange, momentary feeling rather than a possible rite-of-passage. Many of us put it aside and return unaffected to the mind-numbing state of our daily routines.

We have many responses to choose from. We may enjoy the experience, ignore it, fear it, or be thrilled by its sheer grandiosity. The Grail stories tell us, however, that we must spiritually do more. We are required by our own nature to question its meaning, thereby initiating a personal quest to find answers that will heal both ourselves and the world around us. The Grail experience can be likened to a conscious connection to the great Mystery of existence. It presents us with an invitation and a deeply spiritual choice. Do we stay where we are, or take that first step to where our spiritual journey begins?

If we respond correctly, we find the spiritual basis for all the values that Chivalry-Now extols. This inner acknowledgment contributes to our perceptions and guides our actions. By adhering to the awareness of the Grail inside us, we learn deeper truths experientially, every day of our lives.

Here we find the authenticity of life that Western spirituality offers. This happens only when we are open to truth as it daily reveals itself.

Our hero was not open to this at first. Only when he learned how the world suffered from his lack of interest did he commit himself to rectifying the situation. He asked the proper questions. He learned. He lived a brave and virtuous life, and the world was a better place because of it.

How could it be otherwise? There is no doubt that we are surrounded by a Mystery that we cannot understand, despite our accumulated knowledge. The life that informs us is part of it. The Chinese call it Tao, while wisely acknowledging that the Mystery itself remains nameless and formless.

And so it is.

We do not profess to have all the answers on the subject of spirituality. The beauty of the quest is in finding them.

With that in mind, Chivalry-Now does not ask us to believe anything that is unbelievable or rooted in the appeal of arcane sciences. Our premise is that truth is there for us to find whenever we look for it. Once found, actions must follow.

# Chapter 14

# Today's Challenges—*An Exceptional Approach*

**What makes Chivalry-Now** so important for our times is its unique approach to activating the best of humanity at all levels, an approach that expresses the heart and soul of Western idealism.

Rather than propagating a herd mentality to homogenize society into some dull-witted uniformity, its purpose is to inspire us to think for ourselves. It calls upon our capacity of reason to learn through experience and self-discovery.

Chivalry-Now's foundation incorporates valuable insight from the past without inhibiting creativity through unbending rules. It validates the importance of the individual to resist the forces of exploitation. It concerns itself with the future by prospectively encouraging and preserving what is best in human nature for future generations.

Those of us in the Chivalry-Now fellowship never claim that the path is easy. The deeper quest does not cater to those who want truth handed to them on a platter, even if that platter is the Holy Grail. *The Grail itself, like any relic, is not as important as our response to it.* Our very nature calls us to search for truth and relate to it as best we can. That is what the quest is all about.

For this reason we never tell people to *follow* Chivalry-Now. That would suggest that truth is something outside them that can be followed. We do not proselytize for any political ideology – which would be the opposite of our intent.

Instead, we encourage people to question shallow-thinking and feel-good promises. If you need to be a *follower*, there are many groups out there that are willing to exploit you. Hopefully, that will never happen with us.

The intent of Chivalry-Now is to serve as a catalyst for liberation. Whether or not you want that liberation, or are committed to work for it, is entirely up to you.

Modeling itself on the quest, Chivalry-Now guides us more by intuition and personal initiative than any set rules. The 12 *Trusts* are more like affirmations than commandments to be obeyed. They have no power in themselves. We give them power in the way we respond.

Chivalry-Now connects to the wisdom inside us, wisdom that comes to life when conscience unites with our capacity for reason. When we do that, the quest is no longer a concept that is separate from us. It reflects who we are by incorporating the search for truth into everyday experience.

It is important to recognize that culture, tradition and education facilitate the process of human growth. We are not starting from the same point as our earliest ancestors. Instead of us groping in that original darkness, the light of those who came before us illuminates our path. This light is our inheritance, ready for the taking. It provides us with a magnificent foundation of genius upon which to build. Each of us will add something new.

To preserve freedom of thought, which is essential to personal authenticity, Chivalry-Now takes care to rise above two dimensional partisanship and political extremism, where values are decided by party distinctions. It insists that each of us can do far better just by thinking for ourselves.

Chivalry-Now does not ask us to believe the unbelievable, or base our resolve on unproved suppositions. Quite the opposite. It encourages us to delve into our own nature, see things as they are, and engage in life directly in order to learn from it.

Chivalry-Now is realistic. It does not tell people to love one another without reason, or just for the sake of harmony. Instead, it shows us how to make ourselves worthy of being loved by the way we live and treat people. It tells us to develop ourselves as good citizens by applying reason to the moral dictates imbedded in our DNA.

Chivalry-Now takes a sensible approach to human development. Respecting freedom, it presents high ideals not to restrict behavior, but to inspire and support what is good in us already. It understands that no one is or ever will be perfect. Sometimes our best intentions succeed. Sometimes they fail. The important thing is to do our best, learn from failure and try again.

Chivalry-Now warns about the risk of using reward and punishment as behavioral guidelines. Reward and punishment can be very effective at restricting behavior, but only at the cost of disconnecting us from our original impetus to be good. Conscience is not related to reward and punishment – which can, indeed, cripple it. It can, however, be restrained by selfishness, which is exactly what reward and punishment naturally propagate.

Chivalry-Now teaches us to honor and preserve what is good for its own sake, not because of the reward it brings, or the pain we can avoid. This is the thrill of chivalry and the way that we fortify ourselves from the conflicting values that plague society.

Chivalry-Now envelops the complete experience of life – intellectual, moral, and spiritual. It offers personal fulfillment – and not through the artificial means of accumulating wealth, or rejecting desire, or submitting to some cult or charismatic leader. It concerns itself with authentic living. It calls us to be warriors for truth, builders, explorers, protectors.

Chivalry-Now encourages strength in order to change things for the better, to live unafraid, to fight for things worth fighting for, and enjoy the kind of blessings gained from living rightly. Strength is often deemed suspect, and for good reason. It is easily abused. The higher calling of strength is to follow the hero's path in sanctifying the world with purpose and meaning, not destroy or conquer it.

Despite its respect for strength, Chivalry-Now has no disdain for weakness. It tells us to defend those who cannot defend themselves. It supports just causes that assure equal treatment. Power without justice is like strength without compassion – a halfway measure begetting halfway results.

\* \* \*

**King Arthur had no** idea how good he had it.

He certainly faced many dangers: Foreign armies, traitors, giants, dragons, the occasional magician. The risks never ended, but he overcame them all.

How did he do that? According to legend, he enjoyed certain advantages.

First of all, Arthur earned the love and loyalty of his people through generosity, fairness and the goodness of his heart. His reputation attracted the finest warriors of the known world into his service. By extending mercy, he often turned fallen enemies into friends.

Supplementing those personal attributes, legend tells us that he had *Merlin's* sage advice, an enchanted sword and a magic scabbard that protected him from harm.

He had the *Knights of the Round Table* as his Companions, strong and true and devoted to chivalry. Loyal as they were, each was his own man following his own personal quest, while serving justice and the creation of a better world.

He had *Camelot*, a golden city that flourished under his rule that became the envy of all the kingdoms.

For spiritual inspiration, he had nothing less than the *Holy Grail*.

All-in-all, he had quite a formidable ensemble!

But where does that leave us as champions of a new chivalry?

Not as bad off as you might think.

We have no Arthur to lead us, but we have his inspiration.

We have no Merlin, but the accumulated knowledge we do have dwarfs the sum of learning from all previous generations combined. We not only enjoy some of Merlin's legacy, but that of Freud and Einstein and Jung, and thousands of others. We need no arcane crystal ball. The Internet is far more accessible.

It is true that we have no magical swords or scabbards to carry into battle. What we have instead is the pen, long reckoned to be mightier than the sword. We also have millions of people hungry for change, thanks to the disappointing failures of an uninspired status quo.

Arthur's reputation gathered the finest heroes that chivalry ever produced. We have an ever-growing fellowship of Companions as well. They may not be led by the charisma of some hero-king, but they have something just as good – the light of chivalry that radiates from their souls.

Our combined potential is greater than our dreams.

We have no Camelot, but neither did Arthur when he began. The new Camelot is something we must build, something far more permanent than the original.

Spiritually, we are inspired by the same Holy Grail.

How is that possible?

The Grail we search for, the Grail we follow, the Grail we see in glimpses everywhere we go, is the same attraction to goodness, life and truth that Arthur's Grail represented.

As we consider the absence of Arthur himself, we face a deficit difficult to replace. Perhaps our chivalry would be greater if some destined leader like Arthur showed us the way.

Or would it?

I suggest that the grandeur of such a leader is ill-fitted for the democratic challenges we face today. The answers we seek are not those of a king to follow. They come from inside us as individuals, while facing personal and global challenges on our own. Every age carries new trials. Today's cannot be met with a sword, shield and plate of armor.

Our truest enemies are not fellow human beings, but the illusions that pull us away from Nature's Law, and from each other. The magicians we face deal more with marketing and political strategy than spells and incantations. Dragons are nothing more than personal neuroses that compete against what is true.

Whereas Arthur had military skills to push back hordes of invaders, our challenges are different, requiring a different skill set. We need to learn why disgruntled workers or frustrated students express their pent-up rage by sporadically killing innocent people. Or why corporate CEOs risk the well-being of the world to enhance their profits. Or how so many elected politicians, citizen leaders, dare to propagate false claims for the sake of power, and get away with it.

Many of our gravest threats arise from failed political systems, ethics based more on greed than fairness, business and entertainment industries that will do anything to exploit us for money, and a culture that fails to teach anything better.

Bombs and bullets are not the answer. Only the energies and best intentions of us all can provide the answers that we need.

# Part II

# A Practical Guide –
## *Applying Chivalry-Now to Everyday Life*

Chapter 15

# The Franchise of Knighthood
## – Noble Stature

**Reading about chivalry,** we sometimes encounter the word *franchise* listed among knightly virtues.

The more common usages of that word, such as the right to vote, or contractually using a trademark for business purposes, have little relation to its chivalric context.

The definition of franchise relevant to chivalry meant *noble stature*. Its etymology stems from the Anglo-French and refers to freedom, liberty, or immunity from servitude. More precisely, it meant the special privileges of freedom and certain rights granted to those of noble blood. While peasants could also hold and use land as provided by a given lord, the idea of *franchise* recognized a special autonomy given to those who were thought capable of using it properly.

Persons or groups were awarded such autonomy by governmental powers, the aristocracy. It was not an arbitrary gift, but a recognition of station and value to the realm. The person had to be deemed worthy of it. This demanded qualities that would hopefully restrain a person from the abuse of power. *Noble* qualities.

A similar franchise was given to knights as well. A knight was expected to be of noble stature in thought, word and deed. His manners and values should not be trivial or common. These included honesty, loyalty, self-control, moderation, generosity and a strong sense of justice.

According to one dictionary, franchise meant *nobility of mind, liberality, and magnanimity*. These well reflect the knightly qualities that we focus on. They also describe the free spirit of the knight-errant, wandering the countryside in order to right wrongs.

For Chivalry-Now, franchise represents an important melding of freedom and responsibility. When we have sufficient quantities of both, we achieve an autonomy of thought and deed that rises above social expectation, allowing us to critique our obligations according to a higher conscience – previously described as Nature's Law.

The authentic life does not make one immune to the obligations of civil law. What it does is forge an allegiance with something more substantial and fundamental. When we talk about *autonomy* we mean freedom that comes from a melding of virtue, reason and conscience.

If we limit our reasoning to false ideologies, clichés or stale arguments from the past, we constrain ourselves to the limits of regurgitated thinking. We choose this conclusion over that for all the wrong reasons, rather than basing it on actual truth in the living moment.

We must never limit ourselves to being echo chambers of someone else's thoughts, or cogs in a machine. The hallmark of the Western mind is rooted in the actualization of freedom, not some declaration of "being free" while our souls are not.

For the purposes of today's knighthood, franchise means the following:

- Noble stature, including strength, courtesy, just behavior and defending what is right. (By stature we mean that one should be able to recognize an exponent of chivalry by one's character, appearance and civility.)
- A responsible person who is not a slave to ignorance or false ideologies. (Someone liberated from today's consumer-driven conventions.)
- A free expression of conscientious autonomy in one's life, as dictated by Nature's Law and experienced directly.

In other words, the noble stature of today's knight gathers together all the qualities of knighthood and expresses them personally.

Despite a variety of individual differences, there should be a commonality among all true knights that reflects their mutual commitment. They are distinguished by aspects of character that include a dedication to truth and what is good, courtesy toward all, proper etiquette and hygiene, eyes-open loyalty, reliability, fairness, self-control, an even temperament and the avoidance of greed. At all times they represent the values of chivalry and uphold the integrity of their calling.

These requirements are not extraordinary, but they illustrate how comprehensive the commitment to knighthood is. There are no *part-time* knights. This vocation is not about wish-fulfillment or fantasy reenactment. It is engaging in life with the seriousness of life itself.

To paraphrase Edmund Burke once again, the knight *does not trifle with his existence*. Through his ideals and the quest that moves him, he treats the meaning of life with the respect that the miracle of consciousness deserves.

When it comes to the integrity of our life principles, we cannot serve two masters. It would be indefensible to build a chivalric façade around values that are less than worthy of our ideals. Society already suffers from a spiritual schizophrenia of conflicting values. Knighthood must stand as an unblemished alternative to society's spilt personality. It requires that a choice be made – encompassing a rite-of-passage that rejects compromised ideals.

In a world of darkness, today's knighthood offers a unique commitment to a way of light.

# Chapter 16

# Today's Knightly Behavior

**Advocates of chivalry bring** their values to life in the way they act and treat other people. Their confidence is derived from compassion, intelligence, mastery of self, and the kind of humility that allows conscience to adequately merge with reason.

Of course, everyone expresses that differently. The quest produces distinct individuals, not clones. That freedom lies at the heart of this makes our personal responses to life very human, expressing unique insights and decisions instead of memorized reactions.

As one might expect from any cultural ethic, certain courtesies and behaviors should be cultivated. In this chapter, we will examine some appropriate behavior for today's gentleman.

This is not an attempt to homogenize people according to prescribed rules. Our primary inspiration must always come through a direct relationship with Nature's Law within the context of a personal quest. Nevertheless, courtesies and manners that were developed by those before us who engaged in similar quests deserve consideration.

Because Nature's Law, in the form of conscience and reason, provides a curriculum that completes us as human beings, there should be no surprise that it produces similar results in different people. We are all human. Traditional courtesies and other examples of polite behavior reflect our shared humanity.

On the other hand, we must never be deceived into thinking that what appears to be courteous behavior is always genuine, or does not comes with a price. The world we live in is saturated with a thirst for exploitation. Illusion and outright falsehoods have long been used to acquire profit. We should not be fooled by those who hide their intent with false smiles and words of friendship.

Likewise, if our actions fail to express our own inner values, no matter how innocent or positive they appear, they do not rise to the esteem of chivalry. We need to be aware not only of the motives of others, but our own as well.

At one end of the spectrum we have the aspiring knight expressing his ideals in good faith as best he can. At the other end we have the scoundrel who uses courtesy for deceptive or even criminal intent. In between we have people who use courtesy when convenient – as a social convention when niceties are called for, or as a means to an end.

Since the Age of Enlightenment, Western culture has been based, at least nominally, on egalitarian principles. *Nobility* is no longer a matter of belonging to a certain class or bloodline. The word refers to character and honor in the way one lives. Titles, by themselves, mean nothing. When a person exhibits noble character, tried and true, titles are pretty much redundant. For our purposes, the label of *knight* does not mean privilege. It means a *genuine commitment* to chivalric principles. It can only be earned by the quality of one's life.

The challenge we face in resurrecting chivalric principles will not be easy. Such ideals run contrary to the popularity of ego gratification, ill-begotten gain, and compromised values. Nobility of character represents quite the opposite of many of today's standards, in which scoundrels who take and never give are admired and richly rewarded.

Our respect for freedom and the unique qualities of each person's quest rightly prevents us from dictating *exactly* how a knight should behave. Nevertheless, people in search of hope and inspiration will expect the advocate of Chivalry-Now to behave with courtesy, compassion and intelligence. We will be judged by that.

The following is a short review of how chivalric principles can be applied to our everyday lives. Some reflect traditional views that will seem familiar. Others deal with appearance, hygiene, meaningful courtesies and how to act in public. If anything, they remind us that if today's knighthood is to be real, it must be a way of life. Behavior and appearance naturally reflect that.

(Please note: Being male, I hesitate to speak for women, who are best suited to speak for themselves. I will focus on male behavior, inviting women to glean whatever they find valuable that might apply to them.)

Today's knight will be recognized by:

- attentiveness and genuine courtesy toward others.
- personal competence.
- a notable measure of self-discipline.
- attention to personal hygiene and appearance, while avoiding ostentation.
- generosity of spirit.
- a confidence derived from strength and readiness for action, balanced by prudence.
- considerate speech, measured by sincerity, integrity, and reliability.
- a comfortable display of proper etiquette.

Remember, a knight's chivalric ideals do not so much control or define him as they reflect his activated conscience – which is the heart of chivalry as its best, and the core of personal freedom.

While everyone's quest is different, we can presume from what we know that the quest will teach us all to be less selfish, more thoughtful and giving, and less apt to be swayed by popular opinion. By understanding our ideals, we make sure that our values apply to *reality*. True knighthood, as the quest or Hero's Journey describes it, is a fusion of idealism and reality.

Each is incomplete without the other – one lacks substance, the other lacks meaning and direction. We call this fusion *humility,* which provides the conduit to our profoundest insights.

If we are confident in the qualities that we develop, we will feel comfortable in just about any situation. This is one of the greatest benefits to anyone who understands genuine courtesy and good manners. Our responses will be smooth, confident and appropriate, and therefore reliably strong – rather than awkwardly self-conscious.

Likewise, the bragging we associate with adolescence (which too often extends into adulthood), looks boorish compared to the staid countenance of someone with the poise of real experience. The braggart is tedious to listen to – hardly a model of considerate behavior.

Words that are spoken with soft confidence carry far more weight than those yelled in anger. The thoughtful person thinks before speaking and chooses words carefully. This is the result of clear thinking rather than the blustering of ego. People instinctively respond to that.

## Appearance

If the title of knight means anything, it is this: *the knight represents the ideals and values of chivalry.* For today, that means an evolved form of chivalry that is appropriate for modern times. To some extent, this naturally reflects in one's appearance. One's posture is expected to be straight and dignified, projecting inner confidence. Speech should be clear and concise, not loud or domineering. Physical cleanliness speaks much about nobility. One should dress appropriately for the occasion, iron clothes when needed, brush and floss teeth so as not to be offensive, keep hair well-groomed and finger and toe nails trimmed.

*Humility* precludes becoming a creature of fashion who lives for attention. Modesty shows respect for one's knightly vocation, which should always come before ego. There is no mandate, uniform or formula being presented here. Simplicity, personal taste and reasonable economy provide sensible guidelines for one's appearance.

When the knight speaks with people, he immediately establishes trust. He listens carefully, looks them in the eye, and is truthful without being overbearing or afraid to smile. It is amazing how a smile, when sincerely given, sets people at ease and fosters confidence.

Humor enhances friendly communication, but care should be taken to avoid inappropriateness. Bad taste in humor reflects a vulgarity that the spiritual side of knighthood rejects.

Likewise, crude language should be avoided as a sign of immaturity and poor self control. We must always be cognizant of the world we are trying to foster.

Do not cheapen chivalry through proselytizing. Let it be seen rather than heard. Instead of seeking converts, take opportunities to awaken the conscience of others through your actions, and then answer any questions that follow. Keep your answers simple yet meaningful. And remember, not everyone has what it takes to be a knight.

We must never allow our ideals to look foolish. As representatives of those ideals, today's knight should avoid alcohol intoxication and falling prey to recreational drugs. The personal authenticity that knighthood cherishes comes from confronting the world with sharpened wits and clear thinking. By avoiding alcohol and other narcotics, one avoids the associated risks. No one starts out with the intent of becoming an addict or problem drinker. It just happens over time, ruining the lives not only of the addicts but of those around them. By not taking those risks – indeed, *by proudly rejecting them,* the knight differentiates himself as someone who takes life seriously. That too is leadership.

**Manners**
Courtesies are meant to have meaning. They depend upon the

quality and intent of the person giving them, the context of the act, and how one anticipates that they will be received.

The intent of a courtesy is to show respect and bestow comfort. It says as much about the person extending the courtesy as it does the recipient.

The proverbial act of opening a door for a woman, or for anyone, is a sign of polite respect and service. That this has become somewhat controversial with insinuations of sexism shows how removed we are from simple acts of kindness. Everything is suspect, thus maligning everyone's intent. For whatever reason, some people go out of their way to take offense.

Such accusations, sometimes bordering on paranoia, can make it difficult to freely show respect toward others, which ends up fueling the coarseness of life that we see around us. One might ask why anyone would consider a sign of respect as demeaning when it is meant to be quite the opposite?

Today's chivalry encourages respect between the genders as equals, but goes one step further. It tells us that such respect, if it is real, should be expressed and not just assumed. Respect is a positive response between people that calls for expression, and does much to shape our social behavior for the better.

We live in cynical times where even the best intentions are questioned. Rather than surrendering our values to cynicism, however, we should deal instead with what we have. When someone misconstrues a courtesy and responds unfavorably, an appropriate response might be like this:

"I'm sorry. No offense was intended. I meant to show respect, and nothing more."

The accusation might not end there, to which you can reply: "What you suggest is not what I intended. I apologize if you took it wrongly."

Hopefully, the accuser might learn to be more tolerant of courtesy in the future. If not, know that you responded well without compromising your principles.

Rising to greet someone, especially a woman, is another courtesy in decline that the person of chivalry might wish to revive. Offering one's seat on a crowded subway and helping a stranger carry heavy packages are traditional expressions that were once common.

A firm handshake (not squeezing a person's hand just to show how strong you are), accompanied by a smile and eye contact, is still valued in this society. A flimsy handshake implies disinterest. To avoid a moment of unease, do not shake hands for more than two or three seconds – but do not awkwardly pull away if the other person continues.

A pleasing, genuine compliment is always welcomed and a great way to start a conversation. Small talk is a skill worth mastering to facilitate discourse, but should never be phony or taken to extreme. Appreciate nuance and discretion.

Many people make the mistake of talking to excess. Either they are insecure and trying to prove themselves in the eyes of others, or just enjoy being the center of attention, which forces everyone else to be their audience. This is rude. Never assume that people find you so fascinating that they have nothing to offer in a conversation. Constantly imposing your views or stories shows disrespect for others and turns people off, even when their polite smiles suggest otherwise. This is as true in the board room as it is for family gatherings or friendly encounters.

A better way is to purposely draw those around you to share their views. Ask polite questions, such as "what do you think about this?" Most people enjoy expressing their opinions and talking about their interests. By asking pertinent questions, they will think you a conversationalist of high caliber and look forward to meeting you again. In short, people need to be recognized and included. Anything less is an insult.

The coming of the cell phone at a time when courtesy has long been on the wane has led to a host of new discourtesies for which offenders seem completely oblivious. I have seen couples walking together on a fine spring day ignoring both nature and each other while talking on their cell phones. At restaurants, I have seen adults ignoring their own spouses and children while texting or talking to someone who was not present. My heart went out to those neglected people.

We have all experienced cell phones ringing inappropriately at meetings, in crowded theaters, waiting rooms, in church, during speeches, at grocery stores, even on first dates. No one wants to be distracted by or drawn into someone's personal conversations (which, are usually pretty meaningless). They have their own contained thoughts which deserve to be respected. If you must carry a cell phone, please shut it off when appropriate.

To yet another extreme, we see people using cell phones and texting while driving motor vehicles. There has been an increase in highway fatalities since these devices became vogue. Using them while driving is illegal in many places, and common sense warns us of the danger, and yet we see it every day, showing a complete disregard for the law and the value of human life.

These examples list some of the ways in which we have drifted away from consideration of others. A simple rule of thumb is to remember that being intrusive or domineering is not good manners. Figure it out from there.

## Restaurant Manners

Eating at a restaurant now and then is a pleasure that most people enjoy. It provides time for closeness and connection whereby a couple, family or group of friends can concentrate on each other without worrying about what is on the stove. It is a time to exchange pleasantries and bond friendships. It also provides excellent opportunities to practice one's skills at courtesy.

To brush up on restaurant skills, the following provides a quick review:

- *Arrive on time* when meeting people at the restaurant, especially when you have reservations. It is insulting when you do not, and marks you as irresponsible. You may not get another invitation.
- *Shut off your cell phone.* If it is important not to, switch it to silent signal. If you get a call and must answer it, step away from the table for privacy. Do not intrude upon your fellow guests or other customers.
- Make the event special. *Take your time.* Socialize with those you are with. Make it a fun and interesting experience.
- If you are with your wife or girlfriend, or any woman for that matter, show proper respect for her as an individual and for the important gender that she represents. You can help her remove her coat. Or pull out her chair from the table before she sits. Always let her sit before you do.
- Do not wear a hat at the table.
- Your posture at the table should be comfortable, yet attentive to others. Do not slump in your seat.
- Fold your napkin once and lay it on your lap, the fold facing toward you.
- *Always be polite* to your waiter/waitress.
- If you are on a business lunch or with people you need to impress, do not order meals that can be messy, like whole lobster.
- Wait until everyone has been served before you start eating, unless those who are waiting tell you to start.
- Do not hunch over your plate, or lean on your elbows during the meal.
- Use the proper utensil rather than fingers.
- Use cutlery as it is laid out on the table, from the outside in.
- *Please chew your food with your mouth closed.* Nothing looks more ill-mannered than chewing with your mouth open or talking at the same time.

- Complaining about your food to the wait staff is not a sign of refinement. Quite the opposite. If you must send something back, do it discretely.
- Nervously tapping your foot is annoying and should be avoided. This is especially true in a booth, with someone sitting behind you.
- If you leave the table for a while, fold and leave your napkin on the seat.
- Do not speak loudly so as to disturb other patrons.
- Do not continually dominate the conversation. Show interest in what others have to say. If people at your table are quiet, try to include them. If they resist, respect their preference.
- When finished, fold your napkin loosely (so it does not look unused) and leave it on the table.
- Send compliments to the chef when the food is exceptional. We all like compliments for good work.
- When splitting the check among several people, do not be a penny pincher on accuracy. It makes you look petty. If you estimate in favor of others rather than yourself, you display a hint of *largesse*, long esteemed as a knightly virtue. It reflects well on your character.
- Suggesting that you split the bill evenly is considered good form – unless, of course, your portion of the bill is noticeably higher than everyone else's.
- Pay for your lady, unless she insists otherwise. Be attentive to her. Do not look around at other women in her presence, flirt with the staff or hang out at the bar.
- Leave a generous tip unless you have good reason not to.
- The heart of courtesy is to make people feel comfortable and remove barriers to communication.

It is sad but all too common to see:

- Couples ignoring each other at the table. One may be reading the newspaper, or talking on a cell phone.
- People talking or laughing so loudly that you cannot hold a decent conversation even from across the room.
- Checking out what everyone is ordering because you are paying the bill.
- Loudly complaining about your food or service.
- Going into the kitchen to tell the chef how to cook your food.

Our actions define who we are. Chivalry's attitude toward culture suggests that the courtesy and refinement that we express in our everyday lives help shape the world around us. In this way we fight the good fight in everything we do. In an age that cries out for civility, we must remember where civility comes from: *Us*.

## Home Life

The way you treat those who are closest to you, even in the comfort of your home, including your parents, siblings, spouse and children, presents the truest test of your ideals and self-control. It is easy to be chivalrous to a stranger, if only because of the short duration.

Some men feel that housework is for women. The only home responsibility that they feel obliged to do is mow the lawn and change channels on the television. Even then I have seen women mowing the lawn while the men in their lives felt entitled to do nothing. Too many men expect their wives or mothers to cook, clean, shop, do their laundry and iron their clothes as well. In effect, they exploit and are helplessly dependent on what might be described as the slave labor of women.

Somehow, they consider this *manly*.

How is it manly to take such advantage of a loved one? It is one thing if you suffer from physical limits due to disease, injury or age. But to exploit people due to laziness or feelings of gender entitlement is simply wrong.

It is not uncommon today for men and women to divvy up housework chores. Not surprisingly, the tasks often lean toward traditional expectations. That is certainly okay if both agree to it. Nevertheless, chivalry demands fairness. When a woman is willing to take on three quarters of the work, *it is right for the man to point this out and assume more responsibility.*

Each partner should learn how to do the work of the other in case they need to take over at some point. In this way, neither becomes helpless during bad times.

Always be a proper role model to your children and a faithful partner to your spouse. This is not always easy. Facing obligations when you get home after a hard day's work may require self-discipline, which is another aspect of chivalry.

Taking home built-up frustrations from work and allowing your family to suffer the brunt of them is simply wrong. Using alcohol or other drugs to deal with them is guaranteed to make things worse. One should face one's problems maturely and deal with them.

Always remember to perform little courtesies at home. They make life special, and help those you love feel special too. It is a cost-effective way to bring happiness and feelings of security to all.

People sometimes express themselves poorly to those whom they are closest out of anger or frustration. This results in needless arguments that end up ruining otherwise positive relationships.

Some feel that they have a *right* to take out their frustrations upon those they love. This is always bad form, a sign of ignorance and weakness that should be avoided. Raising your voice in bursts of anger proves nothing other than lack of self-control. Indeed, it suggests that your opinion may be wrong, which is why aggressive coercion is necessary.

When disciplining a child, take a moment to make sure that your actions are not only appropriate but provide a learning experience as well. It should not be about reward and punishment. That propagates selfishness. It is more important to nurture a positive relationship between conscience and reason in the development of a child.

To strengthen chivalry, it helps to find a quiet space in or near your home where you can gather your thoughts, contemplate, pray or just relax. Exercise or listening to music can be a helpful part of this.

## Work

The knight carries his ideals wherever he goes, and that includes the workplace.

This does not mean we must parade around on display, or cannot enjoy relaxed informality with fellow workers. It means that we treat everyone humanely, with fairness, courtesy and respect, no matter what that person's position in the hierarchy. The cornerstone of knightly behavior is to always be honest, reliable and trustworthy.

It is fine to be serious at times, or quiet, a little gregarious, or even silly, depending on the situation and the needs of those around us. Accomplishing our work duties, we should be focused and responsible, making sure that things get done in an efficient, professional manner. We promote team spirit by helping co-workers when necessary, even when we are not technically responsible to do so.

We should not take part in office politics or gossip, siding with one person or circle of people against another. We should always contribute to congenial cooperation and avoid unnecessary conflict. When we see trouble brewing, it is proper to discreetly try to ameliorate the situation.

When we are being paid by an employer to do a job, we should do it well. That is our primary responsibility that we accept in exchange for a paycheck. We are not being paid to start trouble or steal supplies or find ways of avoiding tasks that we do not like.

We have at least some responsibility in setting the tone of the workplace. That means contributing to good morale, teamwork, and cheerfully assisting others when needed.

Some people do their charming best to procure employment, and then, as soon as their probationary period is over, they act as if the employer owes them everything. They may abuse union protections. They may spread discontent to others through back-stabbing gossip. This is morally reprehensible.

Most of us have seen people eavesdropping or conspiring in the corner with other malcontents. For whatever reason, their goal is to garner allies and divide the workplace into opposing camps, or target one unfortunate in order to look superior. They exaggerate or even lie, purposely describing someone else's actions in the worst light possible. The reasons for such actions may include jealousy, prejudice, misdirected pride, or a desire to move ahead without being able to do so legitimately.

These are not the actions of honorable men and women, but of people who are disconnected from their own sense of conscience. They excuse themselves by saying that right is on their side. They are fighting against what they deem is wrong.

While it is right to stand up to evil, even in the workplace, the way we do that is just as important. We should always strive to respond constructively.

If you are the owner or manager of a business, you have unique influence in setting the tone of the workplace. Instead of just concerning yourself with your own sense of power or the bottom line, always remember that your employees are people deserving of respect. Treating them poorly will undoubtedly cause problems down the line, and reflect poorly on you as a manager and as a human being. Instead, help them grow and be happy in their jobs. Give them a sense of personal investment.

Being honest, fair and polite in your dealings will go a long way in fostering a productive workplace.

## Hobbies and Interests

Everyone has different interests, and that includes hobbies as well. Those committed to chivalry are no exception. It is only natural to gravitate toward interests that help fulfill or enhance our chivalric ideals. Some study medieval history and knighthood in particular. Some join the *Society for Creative Anachronism* or other re-creation groups to taste some of that lost world where chivalry came from. There are many groups where like-minded people socialize. Some provide educational activities for the public.

Chivalry-Now attracts a variety of honorable people from around the world. Their interests include history, politics, law enforcement, military science, existentialism, general philosophy, the Age of Enlightenment, mythological archetypes, martial arts, gender relationships, theology, social work, music and a host of others. It is our experience that the quest does not provide cookie cutter results, despite certain commonalities. This diversity is part of our strength, and living proof of our respect for freedom and the individual. What makes life a quest is how we learn from it.

We respond to the quest when we are open to new ideas (and some unfamiliar, old ones as well), learn from the truth that they offer, and then share them with people who are interested. This is how we bring authenticity into our lives and contribute a unique vision to the greater good.

People of few interests, who live just to have their egos stroked, or hoard as many assets as they can, or need to be constantly entertained in order to be distracted from the shallowness of their lives, are people who have not yet engaged life for what it is and for what it has to offer. Chivalry has no meaning for them – *yet*.

## On a Date

It is astonishing how dysfunctional men can be when it comes to relating to the opposite sex. While dating, common sense often goes out the window and the ability to judge a woman's reaction completely shuts down. A façade is raised that tends to hide a man's inner qualities with a conceit of self-importance.

I pity the woman who has to suffer through this on a first date. (Imagine spending two or three hours listening to someone brag about all his exaggerated accomplishments, or his self-determined knowledge of just about everything, or just how great he is.) He may try to impress her with shop talk that she cannot understand, or perform a heated lecture on politics or some other subject of which he considers himself an expert. Or he may hide behind humor, launching a constant barrage of jokes and puns hoping to impress her with his wit.

One must admire the patience of women who put up with this and still manage to be polite. They smile. They nod. They restrain themselves from calling him a jerk – even when they realize that their polite demeanor encourages him to go on. While he is planning a second date, she is quietly preparing to change her phone number and move out of town.

Instead of getting tongued-tied or flustered with desperation, try to consider a date for what it is, an opportunity for two people to comfortably get to know each other. That stops when you make your opinions, your job or your esoteric interests dominate the conversation. It conveys the message that all you care about is yourself, and that you have no interest in the woman as a person at all.

Instead, encourage her to speak about her own life and what she feels is important. Show interest by asking friendly questions. If you really want to impress her, communicate as relaxed equals and show how you appreciate her insights. That suggests far more partnership potential than anything else. Take note of what you have in common.

Most of all, appreciate your date for the person who she is.

Every woman you meet is a universe unto herself. Relationships are about experiencing the expanse of that universe, without flooding it. Be open to her ideas. If they contradict yours, show a desire to understand rather than argue. Do not belittle her view of life (or anyone else's for that matter). She is more likely to listen to you with interest if you do the same with her.

Do not be loud or obnoxious. Do not talk about a subject unless you know she is interested beforehand, and enjoys a knowledgeable discussion.

Dating is the closest thing we have to a mating ritual. As in the wild, the male tries to prove his worth to a female he is attracted to. It seems only natural for him to prove how successful he is, how much money he makes, or how he knows everything there is to know about everything.

A contrived recital, however, will probably not form the connection that you are looking for. During a first date you may assume that you are competing with every man alive, and bragging does provide a measurable effort. You can exaggerate, overwhelm, even lie if it makes you look important.

The trouble is, you also make yourself look like a fool.

Chances are that a woman looks for a partner that she, as a unique individual, can feel comfortable with and rely upon. The man does not have to be James Bond or some other fictional hero. (Even when some women fall for that image, problems erupt once the illusion wears off.) Most prefer men who are friendly, quietly confident, reasonably compassionate, and steadily capable of dealing with life's challenges. They should be honest, hard-working, gentle when appropriate and, most importantly, self-controlled.

Women may enjoy romance, but romance is only meaningful when it references a relationship that will continue long after the initial phase of courtship. Not all men seem capable of that.

Listening intently displays the kind of sincere interest that builds trust.

Do not insult your date by treating her as a sex object, or instigating some tried and true routine that is "guaranteed to score." She is a human being first, with a universe of perceptions that may be far more fascinating than your own. Develop a friendship first. Display the kind of respect that recognizes her as special. In her presence, keep your eyes from wandering to other women. Compliment her. Notice how listening expands your own understanding of the world from an entirely new perspective. At the same time, do not be afraid to share some of your insights. Just keep yourself from overdoing it. If all that both of you hear is your own voice, something is wrong.

Remember, you would not like to be sitting across the table from someone who does nothing but brag or throw out stale one-liners, or obsesses about something you have no interest in. If you would not like that, why would she?

When choosing a prospective mate, studies show that a compatible temperament is the most decisive factor to future success. Nothing contributes as much to a relationship's failure than a constant tension and struggle for dominance. Good partnerships are built on mutual respect and congenial cooperation.

While it is important to take note of a potential mate's temperament, it pays to be mindful of your own. After all, of the two, yours is the only one you have a right to control.

Images of the angry male are popular in Western culture. With very few positive images of manhood available, we fool ourselves into thinking that perpetual anger, no matter how unprovoked, is synonymous with manly strength. It actually reflects the opposite, the frustration that comes from an inability to feel comfortable in one's own environment, which implies weakness. Such anger tends to be destructive rather than constructive. It leads to a clouding of judgment, crude behavior and an attitude of selfishness.

Complaining about and insulting what we do not like is easy. Building something positive that will survive the ages is not.

Unfortunately, the persona of the angry male attracts attention and even seems manly to those who are impressed by noise and posturing. Where it leads is usually disappointing.

During the American Revolution, it was not the mobs rioting in the streets that built a successful constitutional republic. It was the collaboration of well-meaning visionaries with open minds who were able to work and cooperate with one another. What anger they felt by injustice was controlled and directed by vision and a high degree of intelligence. Acting civilized was important to them, and the results were admirable.

Why would a potential mate, or anyone for that matter, want to be with someone who is angry all the time? Even if, for some dysfunctional reason, she is attracted to a childish display of power, no matter how impotent it really is, it will get tiresome very quickly.

The only benefit that comes from perpetual anger is the masking of personal insecurity – hardly a mark of strength and confidence.

The person of mature temperament feels no need to hide who he really is. Self-mastery gives him the security to engage the world comfortably. He sees the world as something to cherish and improve rather than tear down.

Never subject the woman you care about to adolescent temper tantrums. If you become someone that she can rely on, you become someone that *you* can rely on as well.

## Chapter 17

# Chivalry & Politics—*Rising Above Partisan Politics*

*"I was asked if I were liberal or conservative. I said neither.*
*Like our real founders, I think for myself."(Author)*

**We are challenged** to find ways of rescuing our civilization from decades of cultural neglect.

Thanks to advances in technology and the entrepreneurial spirit, those same decades were also economically prosperous. With each one passing, the success of the marketplace continually gained dominance over other concerns. The rise of material comfort flourished as cultural values steadily declined. Laws and constitutions no longer expressed the living heart of a compassionate, intelligent people. They become unyielding guides for control and litigation.

We all know that something has gone totally awry.

Monetary success cannot compensate for a moral deficit. In many ways it sabotages what moral instincts we have by distracting us from what really matters, and by making greed more acceptable

We are inundated by distractions designed to pull us away from any sort of healthy introspection. Trivial concerns gain importance as things of great value quietly recede. Freedom loses its purpose, setting us adrift in a kaleidoscope of shifting promises and amorphous results. Who we are as people comes a distant second to career choices, entertainment and political gamesmanship. Instead of being dedicated proponents of life, whose freedom is secured not by money or power but by personal awareness, intelligence and self-control, we surrender to the mesmerizing drone of commercialism and partisanship. All this sets up our political climate for failure.

One of the crowning achievements of Western civilization is its various forms of citizen governments. We see this in ancient Greece's experiment in democracy, ancient Rome's republic, Germanic forms of jurisprudence – all given new and more durable life during the Age of Enlightenment. Democratic republics, which we now refer to simply as democracies, represent the highest aspirations of who we are as a common people.

Here we find social contracts of cooperation based on reason and inclusivity. Each Western nation expresses its own variation that reflects local preferences. Central to them all, however, are guarantees of certain freedoms and human rights. In modern times, these governments prove themselves surprisingly successful, despite the burdensome bureaucracies that they create.

There is nothing streamlined or efficient about a democracy. The founders of the United States were so worried about infighting, mob rule and the oppression of minorities that they incorporated elaborate checks and balances to keep one group's interests from dominating those of another.

It is important to remember what we often forget. Laws, constitutions, enumerated rights, independent branches of government and regular elections provide nothing more than the structure of a democratic republic. What is essential is something that freedom makes invaluable but cannot force: *citizen involvement.*

Democracy depends on the presumed virtue of concerned, intelligent, well-meaning citizens who reflects a high regard for truth.

A democracy of malicious scoundrels or disengaged, uninformed, or selfish people would eventually, given time, destroy itself.

Our Western ideals for law and government are firmly based upon Nature's Law, a blend of conscience, reason and compassion. To allow a political system to disengage from this source of virtue paves the way to corruption.

What good is a democracy that holds little respect for truth, justice and equality? It would be a government that rejects Areté. A government that sells its soul to special interests, business elites or contrived, small-minded political ideologies is a democracy in form only. When the wrong people are voted into office, as surely happens, corruption follows and the system eventually falls apart.

As individuals and as a culture, we need to ask ourselves if we are propagating the virtues that our government needs to succeed and flourish? Or has greed so distorted everything that the virtues that we claim to hold are nothing but empty shells?

Nowhere is this distortion more evident than in political partisanship.

* * *

**We hear a lot of inspiring** words and promises from political candidates around election times. We hear a lot of lies as well. Which is more disappointing? Outright lies that are plain to see for anyone of reasonable intelligence? Or carefully crafted words and promises, polled beforehand that are ultimately meaningless? Both are pretty much the same.

Despite clever rhetoric, partisanship as we know it is the entrenched enemy of Western ideals. Negative ads, distorted or completely false information, name-calling, channeling the energy of fanaticism by flirting with extremists, trying to divide the nation politically to make unity and cooperation impossible – *these are poisons meant to kill democracy.* That their prevalence is familiar to us all serves as a warning.

Even worse is the abject failure of so many citizens who do not even try to become knowledgeable about both sides of an issue or decipher truth from lies. They vote according to party loyalties, or distracting wedge issues, or for how the candidate looks or speaks, or where they were born, or how much they hate the other side.

Or they do not vote at all. I sometimes think it would be better if people who vote frivolously restrain from voting completely. Their withdrawal might stem the flow of unworthy candidates who are wrongly placed in leadership roles. The only way that democracy can flourish is by informed voters standing for truth, not swayed by lies or partisan ideologies.

Most people inherit their political preferences from those who influenced them at a young age. Along with those preferences, they usually inherit a fixed animosity for the opposing side. Dutifully, they listen to media personalities who best support their opinions, which further hardens their ideological framework until they are deaf to anything else. Animosity mounts as politicians take every opportunity to disparage their opponents, quite willing to play on voters' fear and anger with accusations that are often unfounded. Instead of impressing voters with mature skills of statesmanship, they sound more like children blaming each other for some fictional misdeed.

Partisanship is so adept at this kind of brainwashing of the electorate, that many people are convinced that there are only two artificial ways of thinking about anything: liberal and conservative. They draw a line between them to designate opposite extremes, and place *moderates* in the middle. These moderates are the most plentiful in number, but the vocal, energized extremes determine what direction politics will take. That majority opinions are ignored, in itself, is a threat to democracy.

Are there really only two ways of looking at an issue? If so, why choose liberal and conservative? What could be more contrived?

Have you ever wondered what possibilities have been lost because of those artificial restraints? While fights break out about the size or cost of government, filled with hypocrisy, lies and contradictions, no one seems interested in the honest running of government itself, or the best ways to achieve common goals.

Professional think tanks and strategists generate convoluted arguments, and season them with clichés, diversions and disingenuous talking points meant to stir emotions. The media encourages these incendiary conflicts to enhance their own ratings, no matter how damaging or insulting to the intelligence of their audience.

Everyone forgets that the interests of a democracy depend upon honestly examining critical issues. Without the cooperation of the media and politicians, where does one go to find them?

It is frightening to see how easily closed-minded partisanship disposes of reason, truth, honor and simple cooperation in exchange for a dangerous pathology that would destroy everything rather than give an inch.

And for what? The support of a status quo that thrives on corruption? What sort of end game is that?

For a system designed to reflect popular will, this is a betrayal of the worst kind. If people are led astray by leaders they are supposed to trust, or are systematically brainwashed by the media, or are constantly mired in regional prejudices, then truth no longer plays a role in making government work. Without truth, a herd mentality results that is ripe for exploitation.

Under such conditions, the system eventually breaks down. Wrong people gain power, issuing mandates that have little concern for the public good. Important issues are pushed aside for those that are politically expedient. Allies are embraced who are undeserving. Extremism, which always attracts the loudest, most aggressive and least responsible proponents, overwhelms not only majority opinion, but common sense, further distorting issues and priorities.

In the United States, we commonly hear both sides of the political divide declaring that they speak for the "American people," as if their minority of ardent supporters represent the entire population – which they never do and cannot do. Not by a long shot. While their indoctrinated audience claps, people watching from their living rooms know full well that no one is speaking for them. They feel left out completely. They are then left to vote for the candidate that they dislike least.

Thomas Jefferson noted that a democracy cannot long survive without a thoughtful, educated and interested constituency. What we see today is a mockery of the Enlightenment ideals upon which Western governments were built.

\* \* \*

**To those of us who embrace** the ideals of chivalry a sacred trust is given. We are charged with protecting and nourishing liberty and justice which the history of our civilization has long struggled to create. If we are not committed to that obligation, the legacy will simply be lost. A new barbarity will replace it that may not be worthy of freedom. History is replete with such glaring failures.

Those who would defend the ideals of freedom must always resist and counter the propagation of ignorance, hate, irrational fears, or the denial of equal rights to others. Freedom was meant to liberate, not subjugate. Justice can never be justice if it is based on what is false. Those who think otherwise show where their loyalties truly lie.

The quest that chivalry sets its course upon is not a game or set of rules to follow. It is a serious engagement of personal consciousness that nourishes the finer aspects of humanity, including the refinement of virtue, intelligence and compassion. This cannot be attained if we blindly support the dictates of the crowd, or sell our integrity to self-proclaimed leaders who would do or say anything to gain power, or build roadblocks to positive discourse.

This requires us to think for ourselves, even as we consider the reasonable thoughts of others. It means finding truth even under the handicap of long held prejudices. It places reason over emotion, while never allowing one to eliminate the other. It means finding and implementing solutions rather than polluting the world with infinite problems and complaints. These are the qualities of citizenship that democracy needs in order to survive. Without them, democracy degenerates into the ugliness of mob rule, steered by ignorance, lust, avarice and greed. The results threaten everything of value that Western culture stands for.

Can we avoid this?

Yes. We start by recognizing the basic problem, well encapsulated by the French philosopher Jean-Jacques Rousseau:

*Everywhere we look, man is born free;*
*yet everywhere we find him in chains.*

A careless society is quite capable of forging the chains of its own intellectual slavery. As products of that society, we willingly latch those chains onto a false vision of the world, and then pat ourselves on the backs as patriots for doing so.

We are told that the definition of freedom is nothing more than the ability to do what one pleases, lacking any form or meaning or development.

Is that the kind of freedom worth defending with one's life? Empty freedom? Cheap liberty, whose first embrace is stagnation, easily used to hurt the innocent? When we are true to ourselves, the freedom that springs from Areté naturally carries us forward, not backwards.

Today's culture fails to teach us that we are only free when we liberate our truest selves first. It is not a matter of law or even rights, but of *personal awakening*. We can never be free if our moral centers are not part of the equation. One might argue that a sleep-walker is free, but is that true if his mind is only half awake and not responsible for his own blunderings?

The success of our citizen governments depends on reclaiming the depth of our own ideals. This too is what the *deeper quest* is all about.

We are called to do our part as good citizens, and encourage others to do the same. We can do this by writing to our representatives and making our opinions known. We can hold them accountable in public forums or in published letters. We can partake in committees and introduce people to new perspectives. We can politely challenge friends when they express views that we think are wrong.

First and foremost, however, we must live the values that we say we believe in. The more people do that, the more our culture reclaims the ideals that it was built upon.

Chivalry-Now is more than just a code of ethics. It is a mindset that thrives on authenticity. It questions all things to find their deeper meaning. In our personal search for truth, we are warned away from adopting the prefabricated interpretations of others. *Truth is what it is,* no matter what people say. We have to relate to it and form our own opinions.

\* \* \*

**Just as the 12 Trusts provide** us with affirmations related to our personal quests, they provide guidelines for politics as well. Western politics should constantly reflect the ideals that they were based upon.

Consider how the *12 Trusts* apply to politics:

### 1. I will develop my life for the greater good.

Dedicating one's life to the *greater good* provides the moral foundation for political leadership. Running for office for the sake of ego gratification, or in defense of partisan principles, or to sell books or gain celebrity status, or all the hidden perks of the job, is simply wrong.

Does a particular policy support the greater good? Or does it favor the kind of special interests that end up hurting other people? (Not all special interests are bad.)

The *1st Trust* prepares us to be good citizens by setting our priorities right. Because we are part of the world around us, we are always responsible for the greater good.

**2. I will place character above riches, and concern for others above personal wealth.**

The character of a candidate is important to consider. Character includes honesty, integrity and a certain amount of fearlessness in the face of adversity.

Right now, many of us judge a candidate according to media expectations. Does he or she say exactly the right things, and deftly avoid getting into trouble? What about physical appearance? Charisma? Personal resolve, even when wrong?

I have heard media hosts complain about how a politician should have answered like someone else, or *played the part* better – more or less saying that the response should be contrived, like that of an actor in a play. Cunning verbal ripostes are richly admired, even when untrue. And then, of course, comes the media attention brought about by outrageous comments. Extremists especially like that, always pushing the levels of acceptability beyond the pale. They value rudeness more than truth and civility – which threatens how a civilized democracy should run.

There is money to be made in politics. It often opens doors to lucrative careers in lobbying or other industries. Even though the wages of politicians are often low compared to the private sector, the benefits can be very attractive.

The *2nd Trust* points out that the development of character is far more important than greed. If we seriously advocate for this in our culture, life would quickly change for the better.

Remember: *It is the nature of greed to always be the enemy of conscience.*

### 3. I will never boast, but cherish humility instead.

Humility is a vital component of the open mind. It does not assume that our way is always best, or that others are always wrong. It pursues thoughtful consideration first. It listens. It tries to understand. It recognizes that we are all human and therefore fallible.

Civilized discourse employs the kind of humility that invites an honest sharing of ideas. It also allows the ability to change one's mind. It should be that way in politics too.

Shouting people down, insulting opponents, denying facts that are plain to see, are the actions of a closed-minded bully, unworthy of public office.

### 4. I will speak the truth at all times, and forever keep my word.

Truth does not change for the sake of ideology. Trying to bend the truth or ignoring it completely for the sake of winning or attaining power betrays everything upon which Western idealism is based. *The distortion of truth is an attack against decency and democracy, an attack against us all.* When public opinion is not based on informed truth and honest leadership, democracy is doomed to fail.

### 5. I will defend those who cannot defend themselves.

Political leaders are supposed to represent the interests of *all* people in protecting their rights, maintaining their security, and seeing to their general welfare. In other words, in the arena of public service, they are expected to serve as our champions.

Once in office, however, their perspectives often change. There are alliances to be made for political survival. Phenomenal amounts of money need to be raised, requiring incredible amounts of time. Before long, positions on the issues become malleable in order to please a number of disassociated constituents at the expense of everyone else. Most of these activities neither protect nor advance the interests of people. Quite the opposite. They distract leaders from their main responsibilities, and keep the system broken.

Partisan politics, almost by definition, cares more about party loyalty and the acquisition of power than the greater good. It makes everything that a party does questionable. Carefully fashioned words mask what is really meant. Fears and ignorance are shamelessly exploited.

Leaders are expected to protect those who cannot protect themselves. This is the hallmark of an advanced, compassionate civilization. Unfortunately, the needs of the privileged almost always take precedence. Average citizens remain lost in the background, until needed to be roused for election day.

*6. I will honor and respect women, and refute sexism in all its guises.*

Prejudice, in all its guises, sexism being one, racism and extremism being others, impedes clear thinking and leads to wrong policy decisions. It is a broken conscience mired in moral atrophy.

Prejudice means *pre-judging*. Its conclusions are usually based on someone else's error or ill-intent that we inherit. When we surrender to prejudice, we no longer see things as they really are, but as irrational fears portray them. When a political ideology allows, encourages or even winks at prejudice, it represents what real Western ideals continually reject.

*7. I will uphold justice by being fair to all.*

Maintaining justice for all is part of the social contract that Western governments represent. There should be no question about upholding justice for *all* people.

When a political party finds it expedient to withhold justice or deny civil rights to a specific group, it should come under immediate scrutiny.

And yet it happens, and little is done about it.

### 8. I will be faithful in love and loyal in friendship.

Because of the nature of Western ideals, patriotism means more than love of country, when country is defined by land and specific boundaries. It includes certain ideals and values as well, making it stand out from simple nationalism. Since the Age of Enlightenment, patriotism has included human rights, citizen control of government, and the kind of freedom that protects the individual's pursuit of happiness. We consider it a natural progression of the human condition based on reason and compassion. Patriotism is not only the safeguard of a nation's integrity and traditions, but of its philosophical development as well, which has global connotations.

One is also reminded by this trust of all the sex scandals that perennially arise in politics, ruining what seemed to be promising careers. Why should we trust a leader who does not have the decency to be faithful to a spouse?

### 9. I will abhor scandals and gossip – neither partake nor delight in them.

It is a scandal in itself that today's political machine, in symbiotic relationship with the media, thrives on spreading rumors and generating scandals that purposely distract the general public from a cooperative governance. One good scandal will overshadow important issues for weeks at a time on the nightly news, depriving citizens of information that they desperately need to know. This forms another roadblock to an informed democracy.

We must not allow the cynicism caused by rumors and

scandals to distract or dissuade our involvement with politics and other issues at hand. We need to make clear to political leaders and the media alike that we reject journalism based upon sensationalism and crude exaggeration as corruptive. As grownups living in the real world, our concerns must always be far weightier – as theirs should be as well.

### 10. I will be generous to the poor and to those who need help.

When political opinions reflect an *I don't care about others* attitude, they separate themselves completely from the ideals of chivalry, which is an ethic based on generosity (largesse) and service to others.

There has always been a selfish, intransient undercurrent in the West that looks down upon those who are unsuccessful as if they were somehow unworthy of consideration. This harsh outlook found its philosophical voice in Social Darwinism and Calvinism. The Protestant work ethic suggested that anyone can rise to wealth if they work hard enough, no matter what their skills or talents or opportunities, despite the rational unlikelihood of such claims. If they do not, something is fundamentally wrong with them. Failure is seen as a judgment from God, just as success is seen as God's favor. One might view this as a form of self-congratulation by those who succeed, which simultaneously demeans those who do not. It is no surprise that the *inappropriate anger* that often accompanies that attitude resembles a sense of guilt trying to justify itself. They know better in their conscience, which they must then deny.

They proclaim a level playing field that simply does not exist. Yes, people are considered equal insofar as they are human. They deserve civil rights and unbiased justice. Beyond that, however, people are complexly not the same. Neither are the circumstances that they inherit. Success and failure are often decided by factors outside of their control.

Should we turn our backs on fellow citizens because of those differences? Or should patriotism demand that we help them instead? If not patriotism, what about religious belief, or the simple dictates of compassion?

The Age of Enlightenment's emphasis on reason and compassion not only instigated our modern forms of government, it expressed the rational conscience of Western Civilization, promoting tolerance and better conditions for the poor and infirm, and even those incarcerated. (Cesare Baccaria's book of legal and prison reform, *On Crime and Punishments*, published in 1763, was highly influential throughout Europe.) While this movement reflected the moral principles of Judeo-Christian morality, it also expressed the rationale of Nature's Law. Today's Western nations sprang from this tradition. Politicians who pull away from it now, and there are many, revert to *pre-Enlightenment values*, i.e., those akin to the Dark Ages.

**11. I will forgive when asked, that my own mistakes will be forgiven.**

The animosity expressed in today's politics presents itself as an irrational, on-going feud rather than an intelligent discourse of differing viewpoints. Why? Because the strategy of parti-sanship is to propagate itself by purposely dividing nations through conflict for political gain. In such an environment, it is only natural that moral principles are lost, questionable alliances are made, and the general welfare of average citizens is ignored for the good of the party and their funding sources. This attracts the support of unscrupulous people who each demand their pound of flesh.

The only way to break this cycle of contention and work together for the greater good, is to put animosities of conve-nience aside and build well-meaning cooperation. This means forgiving past offenses while rejecting the strange dynamics that caused them. Forgiveness allows us to start anew.

## 12. *I will live my life with courtesy and honor from this day forward.*

Perhaps it is natural for the competitive tension between political opponents always to be strained and leaning toward disrespect. The desire to win at any cost makes them forget the importance of honor and civility, despite lip service to the contrary. When winning is the only objective, dirty tricks are accepted as a legitimate part of the game.

Unfortunately, politics is not a game. It involves the well-being of people, nations and the whole planet. Leaders who seek attention through coarse insults and disrespect not only add to the daily bedlam, they are contributing to our political demise. The courtesy, intelligence, and honesty that provide the bedrock of democratic ideals are replaced by farcical, anti-intellectual discord, that could very well lead to the decline of Western civilization.

We see it happen every day.

All our power, wealth and resolve ring hollow in the moral deficit of partisanship. And the stakes could not be greater.

We cannot wait for some new King Arthur to save us. Our world no longer breeds such giants. We have to do the work ourselves – each and every one of us, in whatever small or large way possible.

The hero inside us calls for action.

\* \* \*

**What criteria should** we use when deciding to support candidates for national office?

On the surface, we should look for honorable people who are intelligent, well-meaning, who can speak well, and have an appropriate presence. They should be scrupulously honest and refuse to pander to fringe elements at the expense of public concerns. They should be flexible enough to change policies midstream if the situation warrants it, and not sink the entire ship-of-state for reasons of pride. They should be able to admit mistakes and make efforts to communicate honestly with their constituents.

We need leaders who represent the very best of our Western ideals – not two-dimensional ideologues who are interested only in protecting ideological purity or the status quo.

This is where the guidance of the *12 Trusts* can play an important role.

## Chapter 18

# Knighthood

**Now that we have** a deeper grasp of what Chivalry-Now is all about, it is time to consider the appropriateness of a new form of knighthood for the twenty-first century.

What purpose would it serve in this age of cynicism? Would it be taken seriously? Are we trying to recover the glory of an age that was never as glorious as we like to think? Or are we wasting time with another form of escapist fantasy?

To have any real significance, knighthood has to be more than an honorarium one attains through membership or dues. It is not about impressing people with an archaic title attached to one's name. If that is the best we can do, why bother?

On the other hand, the world has desperate need for people of uncommon virtue and valor, who exemplify our ideals in action. Society needs people who have arisen from their quests, astute and dedicated, capable of inspiring the masses toward authenticity. It needs honorable mentors and teachers, advocates for meaningful freedom, exemplars of justice and courtesy whose questions and open minds awaken the Mystery in us all.

Today's knighthood is not about a title or special privilege. It is a solemn, personal commitment to action and self-development for the greater good. Its purpose is to produce men and women of impeccable moral behavior, dedicated to liberating people from the spiritual stagnation of ignorance, consumerism and rank partisan ideologies. They would be truth-tellers; visionaries; mentors; volunteers; advocates of civility; exemplars of abundant life; leaders who show others how to reject the trappings of greed.

Such knighthood needs no hierarchy or ritual to prove its

value, no reference to pedigree or alchemical secrets. Those are just distractions. Its fellowship would be based on reality, not fantasy. Members would learn from and encourage one another as they live their ideals in everyday life.

Today's true knights will have found and established their innate moral centers. They will not *follow* a code of chivalry. They will bring that code to life in the way they live as Nature's Law presents it. Knighthood is not about role-playing. It is the shedding of one's old life for something new – and surprisingly not new at all. It is the fulfillment of one's original nature.

The qualifications for knighthood include:

- Personal sincerity.
- Thoroughly understanding the tenets of chivalric ideals.
- Establishing a personal code of behavior that reflects an activated conscience.
- Leading an exemplary life according to that code.
- Being faithful to one's personal quest.
- Advocating for and contributing to the propagation of chivalric ideals.
- Maintaining a positive relationship with one's fellows.
- Upholding the sanctity of truth.

Life-experience helps, including volunteer work, military service, a career in assisting or protecting others, familiarity with the philosophy of the martial arts, support for good causes, and relationships based on genuine concern and courteous behavior.

We have no Arthur to lead us – yet it is possible to march to the echo of his beat. We can do that because the cadence of chivalry springs from the repository of virtue that we all hold common in our souls.

Do you feel drawn to the authenticity of knighthood?

If so, you can attain it by *living rightly*. Follow your informed conscience. Learn and study. Speak the truth and let it be heard in the presence of what is false. Softly. Firmly. Convincingly. Unafraid. Let compassion for all guide your every word and step.

The following essays will shed further light on your path to knighthood.

## Autonomy

**When we think of the knight-errant,** we think of someone who follows the authority of his own heightened conscience as he proceeds through life on his daily quest. We refer to that as *moral autonomy*, which worthy independence is all about.

*Autonomy* refers to a self-determined governance, an earned sovereignty that frees a person from external restraints. It means owning the right and capability of making free choices. It means thinking for oneself.

This does not imply that everyone is automatically a law unto him- or herself. That would lead to chaos – one person's arbitrary rules conflicting with another's. There is an important factor that one must achieve before such freedom can be had. *Areté* – that combination of reason, conscience and virtue that provokes human excellence.

The German theologian, Paul Tillich, explained it well:

*"Autonomy means the obedience of the individual to the law of reason, which he finds in himself as a rational being."*

Obedience to the law of reason just happens to be a fine description of integrity, which includes completeness that is morally sound.

Autonomy works best when it is governed by forces arising from the individual that lean away from chaos. The open, intelligent mind, expanded by compassion and moral virtue, self-discovered and self-defined, is capable of an autonomy that is responsible not only to itself, but to others as well.

This makes perfect sense when one remembers that humane

responsibility is an integral part of freedom.

In contrast, when a good deed is forced, or performed to avoid punishment or seek reward, it lacks the substance of real virtue. A certain amount of autonomy is required to make an act virtuous. Even when one is expected to obey a directive given by someone else, if that directive is not morally based, it should not be obeyed. The responsibility that existentialism insists upon is clear about that.

One's values are often shaped by the influence of other people or by a social environment that pressures one toward certain beliefs. Some never question the values that they inherit because they identify with them. Even when those values prove wrong, they view any sort of course correction as threatening.

They may see their resistance as an expression of personal autonomy. But is it?

Paul Tillich might say that moral autonomy is lost when it fails to include the law of reason on which morality is based. Real autonomy can never be a slave to other people's thinking. It expresses itself through independent choices that are intelligently considered.

Authentic human beings tend to challenge social values that they consider wrong. This is an important part of our spiritual evolution. The inability to defend what is right and change things for the better leads to regression, which then leads to personal and social decay. Justice falls by the wayside from a lack of unbiased inquiry. Truth becomes something we shape according to preferences rather than facts. Courtesies lose their meaning. Peer pressure distracts us from our natural sense of fairness.

Autonomy depends upon personal authenticity. We find it expressed as the *road less traveled,* or as the *Grail Quest,* a common theme in countless mythical stories. We recognize it in rites-of-passage that convey the responsibilities of adulthood.

Autonomy has its limits, of course. Our choices are always

limited – as is free will and our capacity to understand.

This raises a question. If we are creatures determined by our past and limited by our potential, *what meaning does autonomy have?*

Limited as it is, autonomy plays an important role in the lives of those who achieve it. It allows us to challenge the forces of determinism and use reason to liberate our highest aspirations. We are *true* to ourselves when we *think* for ourselves, when we steer away from the trappings of *group think*, and judge the world of values on our own.

Despite the marketing ploys of commercialism, we know that it is impossible for us to *have it all*, just as it is impossible to consistently live up to our own ideals. The most we can do is do our best and aim in their direction.

It is in this purposeful aim toward integrity and improvement, born within our hearts, that we achieve any sort of real autonomy.

## Beyond The Golden Rule

**"Do unto others** as you would have them do unto you."

The *Golden Rule* has long been recognized as the core principle behind all our moral values. Just about every culture and religion offers some variation of it.

A number of respondents to our Chivalry-Now surveys referred to the Golden Rule when asked to define chivalry – and for good reason. The two are intimately related.

What makes them differ is that for chivalry, the Golden Rule is not a goal but a starting point. It prompts questions that are implicit in the rule itself:

- How do I want people to treat me, so that I know how to treat others?
- How do I use that knowledge for the betterment of the world?

- Do my actions fulfill my side of the bargain? Or do I still expect preferential treatment?

Such questions lead directly to the heart of the Golden Rule, where reason and compassion converge as Nature's Law.

Chivalry then takes it one step further:

It tells us to treat people *better* than we expect in return. This is the next logical step in our moral evolution.

Think of how we could improve gender relations by being more than just reluctantly cooperative partners, measuring our efforts to maintain a strict, artificial balance. Think of how our careers might flourish if we did more than the minimum requirements to keep our jobs. If we treated everyone with respect and courtesy, and not just those whom we like, respect and courtesy would flourish. The same with justice and mercy. Since none of us like to be victims of gossip, why not reject gossip altogether? We could be generous to the poor without thought of recognition or reciprocity. We could focus on the greater good in all aspects of our lives, even when others do not.

If we raise our personal goals and live according to the 12 *Trusts*, we elevate the Golden Rule to a higher level.

Here we find the moral instinct that only a quest for truth can teach us – and legends of chivalry point this out. In Arthurian romances, good is often not good enough. Sir Perceval did not meet the requirements of the Holy Grail through heroic actions, for which he was already well proved, but by asking the right questions in order to re-establish health and harmony.

The call to do unto others as you would have them do unto you can be seen as a first step that draws us toward a higher moral truth. It replaces the desire for reciprocity with a deep sense of moral commitment. This is how knighthood differentiates itself from other vocations. The quest becomes a moral gauntlet thrown at our feet, challenging us to develop personal qualities that are continually tested and refined.

In this way, Chivalry-Now becomes more than a code of ethics. It is a drive that develops our complete humanity.

## Golden Rule? Or Iron?

**The Golden Rule provides** a short, pithy maxim filled with practical wisdom. We all want to be treated with respect and courtesy. If each of us extended respect and courtesy toward others, it stands to reason that our own needs would be met. This incredibly simple blueprint promises much for everyone. The appeal is sensible and sound.

But life is never simple. We live in a society where rules that are not so golden hold strong influence.

We have all met individuals who instinctively trample the lives of others. Like everyone else, they want to be respected and treated nicely, but seek to enforce those goals by invoking fear and pain instead. They want more power because they think that they *need* more power. They feel vulnerable otherwise. They follow what might be described as the *Iron Rule: Better to hurt others before they get a chance to hurt you.*

The Golden Rule is far-reaching. It promotes the well-being of everyone by generating friendship and trust.

The Iron Rule promotes a crass selfishness that separates people, generating fear that encourages even more selfish behavior.

Fear has the capability of creating its own self-fulfilling prophecy, resulting in another twist of the Golden Rule: *What goes around, comes around* or *I don't get mad, I get even.* Cruelty breeds more cruelty. In the struggle for power, everyone loses.

You see examples of this in the business world. Where the Golden Rule is applied, humanity is honored and people happily cooperate. Positive work dynamics are easy to maintain, and promote safety too.

Where the opposite happens, people are motivated by fear, stabbing each other in the back. Such negative environments might flourish for a while, but are doomed to fail, spreading misery wherever they go.

So, why would anyone reject something as simple and beneficial as the Golden Rule?

Perhaps their parents taught them to do so. Perhaps some hurt from the past makes them distrust other people. Perhaps they admire some successful person who modeled such behavior. Whatever the reason, they seem ruled by an *instinct to be cruel*. Holding that fear is a prime motivator in human relationships, a source of power. They hone their skills accordingly.

This throws a monkey wrench into the Golden Rule for everyone else. Those who treat others as they want to be treated, suddenly have to deal with someone who does quite the opposite, making an agreeable *quid pro quo* impossible. The assumed contract of cooperative reciprocity is shattered. Why be respectful and courteous to someone who responds with cruelty?

One might hope that the cruel person will learn something through the example of others. Unfortunately, this is rare. Cruel people take advantage of those who do not fight back. All they respect is strength and cleverness.

Some of us admire their energy and efficiency, getting the job done no matter how many corpses litter the field. This loses sight of the greater picture. Even when they use questionable practices for the sake of some worthy project, they lower standards for the future which will bring unpredictable consequences. We end up wondering how things got the way they are.

It is important to uphold our ideals in order to protect and maintain levels of civilized behavior.

By admiring people who undercut the Golden Rule, we betray our culture. Cruelty contradicts the path of reason and compassion. It runs against the path to knighthood.

## Communications

**The life of Benjamin Franklin provides** a fine example of Enlightenment ideals.

He was very much a self-made man, whose interests included writing, publishing, satire, science, religion, politics, and just about anything that caught his attention. It was his personality, however, that contributed to his success. People liked him and took his sage advice seriously. While the diplomatic efforts of others failed to secure France as an ally of the United States, he succeeded and attained celebrity status while doing so.

Part of his success was the result of his talent for communication – something that advocates for Chivalry-Now might want to learn.

Early in his life, a friend told Franklin that he lacked humility. After some honest introspection, he agreed with his friend's assessment. Determined to improve, he made a resolution to no longer make statements that openly contradicted the sentiments of others, or that sounded aggressively dogmatic.

With that simple change he found that his ideas became more readily received. He became more capable of swaying opinion. He also made friends and allies rather than enemies, which made him an excellent proponent for national interests. He was often sought to mediate conflicts and was deemed quite an expert in that role.

While speaking, he would introduce his ideas by saying: "I think," "I imagine," or "Perhaps," and this took the edge off his comments. A bold, declarative statement might be taken as an attack or insult by those of differing views. Instead, he disarmed his opponents by using the tact of an open mind.

In medieval romances, King Arthur was often portrayed as a leader who respectfully anticipated the value of everyone he met. He became famous for transforming enemies into allies. He was not only forgiving, he knew how to make others feel special and appreciated. He understood that honor came not from prideful and noisy arrogance, but from gently changing people's minds.

The king's nephew, Sir Gawain, was well-known for his ability to influence people with simple yet genuine courtesy. For that matter, all of the Round Table Knights were expected to be humble and courteous to others. This was a compelling part of their ability to inspire.

Today we live in a commercially competitive world that has been aggressively divided by political extremes. In contrast, most people are moderate in their positions and tolerant in their beliefs. Extremists represent only a small minority who excessively push to assert their objectives. People who consider themselves completely *liberal* or completely *conservative* are often considered fanatics. That they sometimes manage to assert their views over the majority usually amounts to trouble. No matter what they say, their fixations do not respect the will of the people. Abraham Lincoln once described such leaders as *rule or ruin* politicians. If they do not get their way, they make sure no one else does either.

As proponents of chivalry, there may be times when our conjectures seem to lean toward one extreme or the other, depending upon the issue. Our view of personal responsibility might come across as conservative; our respect for compassion might seem liberal.

In fact, a true independence of thought is not swayed to join either camp. Better to reject the contentious mindsets of extremism and go straight to where truth leads us.

Extremist loyalties form shackles that are contrary to the spirit of the quest. It is only natural for our opinions to change as we live and learn. It should come as no surprise that those within our fellowship do not agree on everything – proof positive that freedom and self-development are more than just words.

As advocates for Chivalry-Now, we need to make this clear when we communicate with others. Our cause, after all, will be judged by how we articulate it. Most people, even some extremists, are tired of partisan bickering. They might welcome an approach that tells them to discard the agenda that someone else gave them, and just *think for themselves*. The greatness of Western culture was not created by partisanship so much as by free and independent thinkers. Common sense places us leagues ahead of conventional political wisdom.

The approach of knighthood is different because our goals are different.

## Extraordinary Deeds

**Chivalry has always inspired people** to perform extraordinary deeds. Acts of bravery. Upholding justice. Protecting and rescuing the innocent. Standing up for what is right, no matter what cost. Confronting evil in its many guises. Defeating proverbial dragons.

What does that mean for us today?

We see no dragons, other than those in movies. Law enforcement officers and prosecutors deal with crime professionally on our behalf. Political leaders are supposed to represent the public interest on a grand scale. Professional armies fight our wars while we safely go shopping. It would seem that the opportunities for bold, decisive, knightly action are simply not that plentiful anymore. In most cases, we are purposely discouraged from getting involved. The system works better without amateur interference.

This lack of opportunity forces many of us to live the hero's life vicariously, through fantasy and entertainment.

We can project images of importance, build our muscles and strut around, but this is only show and we know it. We are left wondering if our leaders are right. Perhaps our only purpose is to make and spend money.

This is the problem we face. In the eyes of today's commercialism, chivalry has lost much of its purpose. While a veneer of courtesy is still important in the business world, and we recognize some value for self-development and higher causes, we viscerally know that something is missing. Our priorities seem upside-down. The function of the hero has become vague, almost irrelevant. Metaphorically, our swords have not only been beaten into plowshares, they have been transformed into plastic keyboards. The quest has been restructured by work station protocols. The most pressing physical dangers that most of us ever face are cigarettes and the build-up of cholesterol.

We find a wonderful depth of meaning in the tenets of Chivalry-Now. But what of *purpose?* What foe or dragon should we be fighting? Without action, chivalry slips into fantasy illusion, just like everything else.

To find the answer, we need to set illusions aside for a while, determine what real threats need attention, and decide on a course of action.

Being a hero no longer means building shield walls or siege engines. It means making a positive difference in people's lives and rescuing society from moral stagnation. It means setting the tone for proper cooperation, protecting human rights, safeguarding the planet, working for peace, and not settling for the dull repetition of inauthentic lives.

The kind of extraordinary deeds that are appropriate for today's knighthood call for an adherence to high ideals in everything we do. Wherever we are, at home or at the workplace, the battlefield calls for heroic action.

Chivalry tells us to be honest in all our dealings and not allow greed to direct our choices. It calls for integrity. Being persistent. Not following the crowd when the madness of commercialism or partisanship overwhelm it. Seeking the inner depth of things. Forging a more complete commitment to love. Having the self-discipline to be gentle and courteous, and yet strong when necessary. We must always defend equal rights.

The sad truth is, what should be commonplace ideals are considered *extraordinary* today. Bringing them back marks the kind of hero that we need.

We can *confront our own personal dragons* – such as neuroses, substance abuse, antisocial behavior, or being inattentive to those who need us.

We can *boldly challenge* bad policies and practices, even when most people support them.

We can *be patient* when everything inside us wants to scream and run away.

We can *deny the lure of illusion* that dares to confuse immorality with virtue.

In the musical *Man of La Mancha*, Don Quixote sings about the *Impossible Dream*. He describes that dream as purposefully confronting challenges, conquering them when possible, and never giving up, even when it leads to death. Chivalry represents the moral capacity for such a dream. It tells us that moral action can never be dependent on reward or punishment, but on the pure and simple premise, as the song tells us, that *"the world will be better for this..."* Here, in this statement of moral truth, unselfish and beyond repute, is where we find our purpose.

When chivalry refers to *extraordinary deeds*, it tells us to live *extraordinary lives* – lives filled with virtue and meaning, so that all humanity benefits by our contributions, no matter how small.

Life does not hand us purpose and meaning on its own. It never has. We only acquire them by our own willful choices.

We cannot believe, as society might tell us, that the man of chivalry is a fool out of touch with reality. We are not well-meaning madmen like Don Quixote. Sanity begins when we see the world for what it is, beyond illusion. One could easily make the case that those who surrender to the deceptions of consumerism are actually the ones tilting at windmills.

If chivalry tells us anything it is this: *we must always be adversaries of deception.* Not followers. Not consumers. Not huddled masses. Certainly not sheep. We must be human beings who boldly confront the world we live in. We will not surrender our autonomy to political ideologies or the ways of the marketplace. *By thinking for ourselves,* we become forces with whom to be reckoned.

Do not think of chivalry as some romanticized code from the distant past. Think of it rather as a personal awakening, a new autonomy based on values that comprise the very core of our being.

Be open! Be enthralled by the uniqueness of every moment! Validate your life by applying yourself as a force for good.

## The Shadow-side of the Male Psyche

**Make no mistake** about it. Following high ideals can be challenging.

While conscience urges us in one direction, we feel something inside holding us back. We may think of this as a conflict of different values or desires. Society certainly supports contradictory ideas. But the difficulty we feel is more than that. It holds a darker element, as if something inside purposely sabotages our best efforts. We seem to be fighting ourselves.

This was certainly true of me.

In my early years, which were usually spent more in solitude than not, I was well acquainted with the workings of my own conscience. You might call it my closest companion. Despite the fact that I had no code of chivalry to reference, I was very much an observer who was constantly weighing right from wrong. This strongly influenced the direction of my life, and often set me apart from the crowd. Even as a teenager, fitting-in and *acting cool* never competed with thinking for myself.

I had no word for it back then, but my moral instincts were preparing me to embark on a quest. I wanted to live a life of meaning, which meant searching for truth in order to be more real. It also meant confronting and struggling to overcome my own faults – which were many.

For example, one of the preferred pastimes in my family was

gossip. Although I was never really interested in that type of behavior, I did partake in it sometimes. I learned first hand how people could feel good about themselves and even empowered while dwelling on someone else's mistakes, problems or downfall. Chivalry taught me to reject that completely.

I had a temper back then, although people rarely saw it. It was internalized. Instead of yelling, I would give the silent treatment and avoid those I disliked. Oddly enough, I could also be very forgiving. I never understood how I could forgive one moment and not the next. While I am much better than I was, I still work on this.

My interests were very closed and limited, and my opinions not very tolerant.

I was an incurable but misguided romantic when it came to women, and made many mistakes which led to a string of failed relationships. At the same time, I learned a few things about what it takes to make a relationship work. Refusing to make the same mistakes over again, I was fortunate to eventually find the love and partnership that I always wanted.

My insecurities as a child were crippling in many ways, but slowly changed during my college years, when books and teachers and new friends opened up the world around me. Nothing extraordinary about that.

We all have our share of personal faults. If we work diligently, we can change them for the better.

But in me, the process was complicated by something else, a persistent discontent that seemed to have motivations of its own. I had no name for it back then. I likened it to an evil persona that lurked behind my every thought and deed. It was very different from who I thought myself to be. I could scarcely admit that it existed. Religious references to "our evil nature" or "sinful tendencies" or "demonic possession" seemed to point to it.

On sleepless nights, of which there were many, I would struggle with this grotesque part of my psyche, sensing its rage and resentment, its intent on striking out against everything good that I believed in. The most I could do was repress it – make believe it did not exist. I think that many of us do the same thing.

As my journey in life continued, my career in social work introduced me to a variety of dysfunctional personalities. I saw people who continually, even predictably, sabotaged their own possibilities for success. I listened to couples who would not budge to fix their relationship problems even when the solutions were fairly simple. I counseled people who suffered from addiction, violence, and sheer stubbornness, and continually got nowhere. Something engrained in their psyches seemed to hold them back from doing what was right.

Something was holding *me* back as well – something that I would have to deal with before finalizing my commitment to chivalry.

*Carl Jung,* the founder of analytic psychology, proposed that deep inside the male subconscious there exists a wild energy that purposely contends with our best intentions. Savage, irrational, easily frustrated and angered, it is quite capable of filling the mind with desires that are completely at odds with our moral beliefs.

Society teaches us in a thousand ways to repress that part of us as something uncivilized and unnatural. Unfortunately, the more we try to be rid of it, the stronger it becomes. Ignore it, and it seethes like a lion always ready to attack. We conclude that the best we can do is channel its rage into appropriate conduits, such as competition in sports or business.

Jung tells us that this dark side of our personalities can never be expelled or completely subdued. It follows us like a *shadow*, which is what he called it, dark and indescribable. Just like a real shadow, it distorts the image of who we are.

It is composed of all the natural instincts that society tells us are unacceptable. They do not vanish as we grow up. They merge together and form a life of their own.

We experience this as personal darkness, filled with a savagery we do not want to recognize. It haunts us when we least expect it – an angry phantom rooted in our primitive core, maligned by civilized expectations and marginalized by our attempts to repress it.

This frustrated shadow is easily capable of subverting our best intentions – not because it is evil per se, but because we are constantly thwarting its existence. By considering it something *bad*, we deny it a proper role in our lives, which shapes it into a monster. Instead of incorporating whatever positive aspects that it offers, which would complete us, we provoke its rebellion through constant repression.

Whether we recognize it or not, this shadow is part of who we are. Without it, we remain inauthentic. Even our embrace of chivalry would be less than it should. We become empty shells adhering to moral dictates that lack true meaning.

One might describe the shadow side of our psyche as the moral tension of having one foot in heaven and the other, not in hell, *but here on earth.* Its wildness reflects our original nature. Without it, personal self-discipline becomes an act, our strength depleted, our connection to the earth, which is the Mother we sprang from, broken. Metaphorically, we become the disappointment of heaven's grand design, severed from our roots and sapped of our virility.

This shadow is part of who we are, influencing our every thought and deed. It either substantiates or perverts our best intentions, depending on how we relate to it. It is our connection to nature, our unrefined edge that distinguishes men from women, no matter how refined we shape ourselves. When we fail to give it a proper role in life, it becomes discontent, brazen, uncontrollable, perverting the virtues that we so desperately seek to honor.

Denying our shadow merely provokes it to wreck havoc in our lives. We wrestle with it, try to subdue it, only to find that the struggle never ends. In this respect, the shadow prevails as a dark influence rather than something that completes us. We cannot suppress it without losing who we are.

Chivalry, despite its focus on refinement, tells us to embrace our wild center, recognize its intrinsic value, and honor it as a natural source of energy – even though it borders on amorality, as things of nature do. It is here where the ideal warrior first takes shape, rising from the earth toward the refinement of his ideals.

How should we handle this?

Chivalry does not ask us to tame or eliminate this wild excess of spontaneity. Quite the opposite. It gives the shadow *purpose and meaning*, channeling its energy throughout every fiber of our being, melding it with everything we do. Through this process, we are made whole.

Our wildness becomes self-destructive only when we reject it or hold it at arm's length. By infusing it into our lives, it nourishes the soul like nothing else can. Our shadow is not a thing of evil and perversion – although *untended*, it can be both. It is an aspect of our deepest identity. We need this shadow to complete who we are. Just as importantly, *it needs us as well.*

In order to transcend inner barriers to chivalry, it is important for us to find our shadows and integrate them into our lives. We might not be pleased with what we find but remember, this is result of neglect, not malice.

Embrace your shadow-self. Raise him to consciousness – and he will raise you to completeness.

There are ways to do this.

Jung tells us that the simplest approach is through *ritual*, whereby we formally recognize and honor the wild man as a valuable part of who we are. He suggests that a self-made ritual is enough to heal the rift – the unconscious mind asks for nothing more. We can make this ritual part of our commitment to chivalry.

To illustrate how simple this can be, the following is paraphrased from my own short ritual. Please devise your own as it best applies to you.

In a quiet place, with no distractions, relax your conscious mind so that it does not form a barrier to your subconscious. Try to imagine your shadow, dark and alone like one who has long been disinherited and exiled. Call to him, and say something like this:

*Dark Man of my soul,*
Come out from the shadows. I honor you this day – you from whom the energy of resolve originates and resides. I praise the honesty of your feelings, rooted in the earth and in battle and in the hunt. Your anger is profound. Your need for action true. I applaud your sense of outrage and need for justice. Without them, I would be an empty shell. You embolden me toward liberation, to live by my own accepted code. You are my father and brother and truest friend. Without you, I would be powerless to resist my enemies or fight for the good.

This sword symbolizes who you are – what you mean to me and also to the world. Strength. Action. Defense. The ability to slice away illusion and destroy evil. It represents the history of man, blood sadly spilt on the battlefield, which connects us all.

Stay with me. Take your honored place in my soul and in my life. Strengthen me with your power. Guide me with your earthly wisdom.

If you perform your ritual meaningfully, you will experience a new wholeness and contentment. Over time you will notice that the resistance you once felt is subsided. At least it was like that for me.

On the other hand, the ritual may only start the process of integration. It may not complete it.

According to Jung, it is possible to have more than one shadow. You may have to confront several. If you find any of this difficult, find help from an analytical psychologist trained in Jungian psychology.

## The Accolade—*Becoming a Knight*

The accolade once served as a rite-of-passage that initiated worthy candidates into knighthood.

Hollywood usually portrays this as an elaborate dubbing ceremony, where the kneeling candidate is tapped on the shoulders by the flat of a sword, wielded by a knight or king who publicly and formally declares him a knight.

While there is some validity to this image, history presents another portrayal, often performed on the battlefield. A knight, sufficiently impressed by a warrior's loyalty and skill in battle, would strike the candidate on the head or shoulder with his hand or fist, and say the words: "Be thou knight."

Earlier references, dating back to second century Germanic tribes, show the leader of a war band conferring arms upon a new warrior as he joins their ranks as a mark of reaching adulthood.

As time went on, the rite became more elaborate and Christianized. It included a bath to symbolically wash away sins, followed by a solitary, all-night vigil in church. The acolyte would attend mass the next morning, and receive a lengthy sermon about the responsibilities of knighthood. Only then did the knighting ceremony actual begin. The initiate would be girded with a sword by his knightly sponsor, who then tied a spur upon his foot. Only then would the striking of the shoulder or head occur that marked his true vocation.

Is it possible to become a knight today?

There are knightly organizations that still exist. A few, like Knights of Columbus, are easy enough to find. The Queen of England occasionally bestows knighthood on select individuals of great accomplishment. The Society for Creative Anachronism has specific guidelines, including combat, that must be met before a member can receive the accolade.

The question arises about some form of knighthood for those of us who advocate for Chivalry-Now. Would it offer some legitimate purpose? Or serve as a distraction?

One young man of impeccable intent thought it best to keep the accolade at arm's length. He feared that just the wanting of it might tarnish the purity of his ideals. His concerns were justified. Whereas the quest is a journey toward a goal that can never be reached, knighthood presents a more tangible goal, and one that is very capable of appealing to the ego.

Why ego? Because it suggests a recognition of special worth associated with legendary heroes of the past. It is only natural to want something like that. Such a desire, however, can also be distracting, and even detrimental to what really counts. It allows ego empowerment to supersede the quest as a prime motivation, producing the opposite of its intent.

As the young man recognized, it is sometimes easier to live the chivalric life without the accolade. Most people who live it fall in that category, which might be called spiritual knighthood. If the 12 Trusts live in your heart, the accolade is pretty much superfluous. If they do not, the title means nothing.

To the true initiate, however, knighthood does represent a thing of great value. Forget the images of rituals and swords and colorful banners. These are nothing more than the peripheral trappings of ceremony. For our purposes, the heart of the matter has to do with a demonstration by the acolyte of personal commitment.

Of course a dutiful commitment in your heart is just as binding, and will bear similar fruit. What matters is the genuine adherence of your commitment to a certain way of life. The accolade is a recognition of this, nothing more.

Take the analogy of marriage. Unmarried couples may live

together in a loving relationship bound only by the full commitment of their hearts. It happens all the time. Relationships are what you make of them, good or bad, lasting or not.

When a couple gets married, however, they make a public declaration of love and commitment that adds a new dimension to who they are. The law sees them as legally bound to this commitment – even though it may still be as solid or fragile as any other. On the surface, things might even look exactly the same as those who live together unmarried. But they are not. A public declaration of commitment is not easy to walk away from. People see you differently. Even the way you see yourself changes. The consequences of breaking your pledge seem far more real.

Knighthood is like that, a public commitment with public consequences. You will be judged by the world for the way you handle your commitments, just as someone who is married is held more accountable for his or her relationship responsibilities.

The accolade also provides a certain amount of legitimacy because it is recognized by others. Because it involves the judgment of someone else, it carries the kind of significance that is true for all rites-of-passage. A person, society or organization recognizes the beginning of a new life through association. In medieval times this cultural acknowledgment granted status, privileges and grave responsibilities. Today, it boils down to formally acknowledging the responsibilities of commitment.

Some consider the accolade a life transforming sacrament from which a new vocation, almost religious, begins. That holds tremendous value in the ritual as well.

The person of truth, however, *is a person of truth*, accolade or no. People recognize his or her qualities because they see them.

Someone's name need not be prefaced with "Sir" to elicit high esteem. Confirmation of personal value depends on actual behavior.

The world has great need for people of heroic character, strong and true, yet humble as well. Each of us can strive to become that.

- We are *knights* when we move from the centricity of selfishness to ideals of greater meaning, thus improving ourselves for the benefit of the world.
- We are *questing knights* when we take life seriously enough to live it as a quest for truth – when our eyes are open to the spiritual qualities of life that can only be experienced firsthand, and not from wish-fulfillment.
- We are *knights-errant* when we freely help those from whom we never personally benefit.
- We are *noble* when our hearts act nobly to all other persons.
- We are *battle lords* when we lead the charge for a good cause.
- We are *kingly* when we so identify ourselves with the well-being of the earth and all those who live on it, that our personal welfare becomes inseparable from theirs. The kingly heart inspires high ideals in other people.

The Fellowship of Chivalry-Now occasionally does bequeath the accolade on Companions of long standing. Many of them serve on our *Council of Knights*, overseeing the direction of our cause. This does not detract in any way from the many worthy people who belong to our fellowship who never become knights, but live their lives in the spirit of true chivalry.

# Epilogue

**One quest ends** and another begins.

You have feasted at the Grail King's table. You have seen treasures paraded in the hall, and asked the right questions. You have learned that the Wasteland, like the wounded King himself, can be healed as a result of new consciousness.

You find yourself a knight reborn, ready for your deeds to be entered into the *Book of Life*. You understand and embrace the spiritual depth of your ideals. Your eyes are clear. You reject the illusions that others would blind you with. The siren's song of greed no longer holds its enchantment. Aletheia has awakened your heart.

The future beckons, and you are not afraid.

You are prepared. You have trained your mind, body and spirit for the challenges to come.

It is time to leave the Temple of Esoterica. You are charged by your own conscience to take what you have learned into the real world, and change things for the better.

Self-sufficient as you are, and must be, know well that you are not alone. A fellowship of brothers and sisters await you at their table, an oasis of like-minded people in a troubled world. The Companionship of Chivalry-Now.

Visit www.chivalrynow.net to learn more.

# Part III

# Appendix

- **Survey Results**
- **Quest Questions**
- **Reference and Review**

# Supplement 1: *Chivalry-Now Survey Results*

In 2007 we held a survey to learn how average people felt about chivalry. We wanted to project what sort of reception Chivalry-Now would get from the general public. The survey did not mention how we were fashioning a new code of ethics known as Chivalry-Now, and so the answers we received were not biased in that direction.

We were pleased by the results, which were overwhelmingly positive despite many misconceptions.

Not all the questions and responses are listed here. A number asked for the respondents' opinions, which would make this section too long. The most notable comments are listed at the end.

*Please note:* some respondents failed to answer all the questions, which is why some of the answers do not reflect how many people participated.

We had 150 Respondents. 65 were men, and 85 women.

**1) Does the word chivalry convey a positive, neutral or negative image in your mind.**

**Results:**

|  | Positive | Neutral | Negative |
|---|---|---|---|
| Male | 51 | 13 | 1 |
| Female | 69 | 12 | 4 |
| Total | 120 | 25 | 5 |

Conclusion: A large percentage of respondents view chivalry in a positive light. Many of those who checked *Neutral* made positive comments later on. Although we anticipated far more negative responses from women, only 4 were given. Their complaints focused on feminist concerns which Chivalry-Now hopefully remedies.

(The following question was preceded by a list of chivalric values, such as Truth, Justice, Courtesy, etc.)

**6) Do you find a focus on these values missing in your life?**

**Results:**

|  | Yes | No |
|---|---|---|
| Male | 15 | 49 |
| Female | 42 | 42 |
| Total | 57 | 91 |

Almost 3 times as many men said **No** rather than said **Yes**. The number of women was equal. It suggests that three out of four men feel that the virtues of chivalry already influence their personal lives. Half of women felt differently.

**7) If you were invited to join a [modern version of the] Round Table today, would you...**

|  | Male | Female | Total |
|---|---|---|---|
| Accept without hesitation. | 7 | 16 | 23 |
| Find the offer attractive or flattering and actively look into it. | 29 | 30 | 59 |
| Want to know more about it first, but only if the info comes your way. | 15 | 22 | 37 |
| Feel somewhat amused, but not interested. | 13 | 9 | 22 |
| Think the idea is stupid, even though it appeals to something |  |  |  |

| | | | |
|---|---|---|---|
| deep inside you. | - | - | - |
| Think the idea has no relevance. | 1 | 6 | 7 |
| Consider it a complete turn-off. | - | 2 | 2 |

The results of this question are interesting. If there were something equivalent to the Round Table today and these people were invited to join, more women would accept without hesitation than men. This may suggest a higher degree of cynicism in men, or a more spontaneous idealism in women. Perhaps both. The numbers come closer when asked if they would find the offer attractive and actively look into it, which represents the largest number of respondents. These are people with their feet on the ground who want to contribute to a force for good, but will not jump in blindly. Approximately the same percentage of men and women want to know more (remember, there were more female respondents), but only if the information came their way. They find it attractive, but are not about to take any initiative. The attraction is there, but not the impetus to act on it. Ten men and six women find the idea amusing, but simply are not interested. Nobody thought the idea was stupid. The last two answers, by far the most negative, represent only five respondents, four women and 1 male. While women responded more positively overall, only a single man was able to turn away from it completely.

**8) How do you view Camelot as a symbol? Which of the following statements most closely resembles your opinion:**

| | Male | Female | Total |
|---|---|---|---|
| It is a valuable ideal that can be used for cultural, social & political improvement. | 27 | 47 | 74 |

| | | | |
|---|---|---|---|
| It has some nostalgic value. | 15 | 11 | 26 |
| As a symbol for change, it is probably too late to make a difference. | 9 | 13 | 22 |
| A nice idea that can have no realistic impact on today's world. | 12 | 12 | 24 |
| Ridiculous to try. | - | - | - |
| I like the way things are, and don't want change. | 1 | 1 | 2 |

Another question with interesting results. Less than half of the men and more than half the women feel that the Utopian symbol of Camelot has value for cultural change. The rest, other than 2, are divided into three categories that seem to regret the lack of possibility for change. They do not say it is ridiculous to try, or that they like things the way there are. Their feelings are positive, yet somewhat defeatist.

## 9) Would you personally like to see men act more chivalrously?

| | Yes | No |
|---|---|---|
| Male | 54 | 10 |
| Female | 79 | 5 |
| | 133 | 15 |

This final question says it all. Most respondents (all but 15) said that they would like men to act more chivalrously. Whereas 30 started this survey by saying they had a *Neutral* or *Negative* impression of chivalry, most concluded that they wanted more of it in their lives. Answering the survey questions gave them the opportunity to think about the concept, and their attitudes became more positive.

## Conclusion

Results from this survey show that chivalry appeals to the majority of men and women, even though they live in a world where such ideals are trivialized or completely ignored.

The majority of female participants want men to be more courteous, but in a manly fashion. They want men to be strong, unselfish, self-disciplined and reliable. There is a small minority who hold residual resentment from the early feminist extreme, but their objections say nothing significant in light of a new chivalry, modified to be appropriate for today.

The males are more difficult to categorize. Their words show an almost innate connection to chivalry. Many feel that they already express chivalric ideals in their lives. They are more cautious, however, when responding to the idealism that chivalry calls for. This may be due to many factors, such as past disappointments, the cynicism that comes with maturity, and doubt that there can be a significantly positive role for men beyond the drudgery of work.

A number of men seemed cautious in their narrative responses, as if they feared that they might be labeled sexist. It seems that their fears are mistaken. What the survey results show is that most women, by far, want men to be more chivalrous.

Both men and women long for a world of grace and civility, where gender roles respect differences while comfortably working together. The tone is one of regret or sorrow because the world is not like that. They want something like chivalry, but cannot see how it can exist in today's world. Nothing in their lives seems to indicate that a majority of people agree with their longings and would welcome change. Our present society seems to tell them that there is no room for chivalry anymore, that people do not want it, or are incapable of it – even though our results show otherwise. Political correctness, the need for a strict but confusing equality among the genders, the dominance of our culture by values centered in greed, seem overpowering. Society has become an economic machine that defines everything not according to virtue, but from a marketing perspective, from politics to religion, to how we value everyone around us. This has had a dehumanizing effect. We no longer see how we can change things for the better, or shape them the way we would like them. We do not even discuss it.

These surveys reveal sadness and longing for something better, something more satisfying and humane than the mindless consumerism we have today.

There were some surveys that were incomplete. The respondents might have been rushed or not really interested. A few (very few) obviously held negative views of chivalry, seeing it as something that demeans women. Others did not know what chivalry is all about. One 37-year-old female defined chivalry as "King, Queens, Knights and a round table, dancing and wine." What she found appealing was "clothes, and manner [of] speaking." She added the following comment: "It would have been nice to go back in time. We only get one life and God chose this one for me."

Some of the genuine concerns that people expressed have already been addressed in the formation of Chivalry-Now.

# Male Comments—Summary

Both genders tend to identify chivalry with attitudes toward women, stressing courtesy.

Many recognize other dimensions too, including common decency, courtesy, self-sacrifice, a code of conduct, integrity, aspirations toward noble goals, bravery, pursuing the high-road, honor, respect, pursuit of an ideal, helping those in need, a more compassionate society, courtship, redeeming the qualities of men, and living ethically and honestly. They thought that a resurgence of chivalry would make for a better world.

A number of men inserted comments suggesting that women should also be more chivalrous. This may be due to concern for equality between the sexes. Some complained that women can be very discourteous, and are in need of a formal ethic. Some feel that male chivalry is dependent on women's attitudes, saying that women make it difficult for men to act with courtesy, by rejecting such acts as opening a door, etc.

All but ten males would like to see men act more chivalrously.

**Notable Quotes from Males** (ages, when available, are noted in parentheses)

I was fortunate in having a grandmother who instilled the virtues of "Chivalry" when I was young. I aspire in everyday life to live the code of Chivalry. All that Chivalry entails is more than appealing, it's the right way to live one's life regardless of what goes on around us or happens to us. For me, there is no other way. (age not stated)

Chivalry is appealing because acting chivalrous make you feel good; it fills you with a feeling of warmth. Warmth given off by a candle of passion of doing good that is ignited and remains ignited as long as you remain honorable and do good everyday of your life. This warmth from chivalrous acts makes chivalry appealing. (16)

Today's "accepted" ethics, if unchecked, will bring about the downfall of democratic society and therefore the United States. (73)

I would also like to see more women allowing men to be more chivalrous. (24)

Many people I know still espouse these values and try to live by them in their day-to-day lives. (57)

It is one of the redeeming qualities of man. (23)

I have been a fan of Arthurian ideals since childhood. Should more people adopt them, it would be a better world. (56)

Camelot is "far" [too] Utopian a term. It does not connote a realistic goal, and it failed. (56)

I believe that mutual respect is one of the greatest things lacking in modern society. (19)

[I dislike] nothing [about chivalry] but for the fact that people of the 21st century have difficulty relating the tales' messages to their current situations. (62)

We should continue to strive for the betterment of our fellow beings. This will take courage and fortitude. (73)

Common decency, courteousness – kindness and thoughtfulness to all. (age not stated)

Courtesy, general good will and honesty and kindness toward others. (age not stated)

Being a good human being. (50)

Chivalry = respect, not domination. Perhaps men think chivalry is a code now outdated, especially since the idea of women's rights and so on. I would say precisely because of that movement (which I applaud), that acting respectfully toward women is even more important. (54)

A human behavior involving respect of others, honesty and courage. I would like to see the radical feminists allow men to act more chivalrous. (55)

Importance of virtues like honesty, good works, courage, humility, respect for women and poor/powerless. (63)

Chivalry promotes the best in people by pursuing the highest expectations in human behavior. Excellent personal conduct and demeanor toward the world and others, which conduct and demeanor is motivated by pursuit of ideals and not by personal gain. I am wary of some people who are prone to be pretentious (who are lazy and (?) would not take the ideals. It's never too late. (55)

Inherent sexism. (21)

Good idea – this subject. (67)

Brings order to male/female interaction. [I dislike] women who demand compliance, and the assumption that women cannot care for themselves. (75)

High moral standards.

# Female Comments—Summary

Both genders tend to identify chivalry with attitudes toward women, stressing courtesy.

Other insights from women include: politeness, caring about other people, doing the right thing for the right reasons, helping people, acting like a gentleman. They seemed positively aware of chivalry, and considered it a male ethic.

One woman (who had a very negative view of chivalry) stated that women are not to be honored, but respected. This suggests her concept of being honored is somewhat dehumanizing; i.e., putting women on pedestals. There is a difference between honor and worship, and we have to delineate that.

All but five female respondents would like to see men act more chivalrously.

## Notable Quotes from Women

The willingness to stand up for your beliefs, hold others and life precious and do it with respect, grace and dedication. (48)

The romantic in me would embrace this idea [that Camelot is a valuable ideal that could be used for cultural, social and political improvement]. (48)

It is the perfect example of living by [the] Golden Rule. (74)

Chivalry is an attitude of selflessness, in which one does everything possible to keep another safe, comfortable and happy. (74)

I dislike the fact that chivalrous behavior is dying. (53)

Seems outmoded – associate with "special handling of women."

Despise "holding doors." (53)

It just feels right. It is an admirable quality. (58)

The choice is to do the right things, for the right reasons, at the right times. Respect, courtesy and honor. (58)

I believe we have gotten so far away from the basic courtesies in life – we need to have high ideals and value of what is truly important in life. I think we have drifted so far from this as a society and it is reflected daily in the news... (41)

...perhaps it [chivalry] could be modified and updated to take into consideration the changing roles of women in our society. (63)

In many ways, we've become a rude, uncivil society, which saddens me. (63)

[The appeal of chivalry exists] as long as it is sincere, not for personal gain. (51)

[What I find appealing] A different time, [when] men were gentlemen. (49)

Young men today aren't usually growing up to be gentlemen... it's refreshing to see men who possess gentlemanly traits. (32)

Gentlemanly traits that a man possesses – politeness towards not only women but mankind, a sensitivity and a possession of duty and honor. (32)

[What I dislike about chivalry] 1) The lack of the expectation that chivalry is the norm. 2) The defensiveness of a man who doesn't portray it. (33)

Please let it not be too late. (58)

I think they [chivalrous men] were self-absorbed. People are often rude and extremely self-absorbed.

The word [chivalry] implies consideration for others. Most men I know are pretty chivalrous. (41)

If the person is being genuine, chivalry, in moderation, is a nice social grace. [I dislike] when someone is overly solicitous. Act, no. Be socially engaging, honest – yes. (52)

[Chivalry is] the Golden Rule being acted out. (54)

The idea of honor and justice and peaceful ways of solving issues. [I dislike] Perfectionism, stress of being perfect can cause anxiety or self-righteousness perhaps. (60)

An outdated love of country – right or wrong. Freedom and justice as a goal to strive for on a personal and global level. (58)

Chivalry is a form of courtesy and kindness. (59)

I think chivalry should also apply to women. (60+)

A guy taking care of me. (16)

A man being polite to a woman – holding the door, standing when she enters the room – making her feel welcomed.

When it's too much, it doesn't feel natural.

It is interesting to relate the thoughts and beliefs of chivalry and compare them to present day society, societal problems and so on. I would be interested in the comparison and how chivalry could help social problems. (22)

Putting the needs of others before yourself. (36)

Especially young men/teenagers. (29)

The promise of respect, loyalty, admiration which is practically nonexistent today. (35)

I believe that today's feminist movement has probably done the most harm to the idea of chivalry in relation to women. Materialism as well has eroded the idea of "doing the right thing" in today's greater society. (32)

I equate chivalry with good manners and honorable conduct. If there were more chivalry, the world would be a kinder place. I'd also like to see women behave in a more chivalrous manner. I think it is our obligation to honor and protect one another, in our daily lives, and in a global sense. (57)

I think there is tremendous value to compare old and new. And "how" to apply in a world with diversity and international context. [Note: this woman claimed to have a negative image of chivalry, and equated the Round Table to the Moral Majority; i.e.: the Christian Right.] (54)

# Supplement 2: *Quest Questions*

The Grail Quest literature is quite specific in its final conclusion. The hero completes what is required of him not by the accomplishment of some great feat, but by asking the right questions in the face of profound mystery. The spark of new consciousness that the questions signify heals not only the wounded Grail King, who represents the leadership of society, but the ills of nature as well. The Wasteland becomes fruitful, and the joy of life returns to all.

This lesson remains significant today. It calls us to a state-of-mind that confronts the mystery of life in a proper manner: humbly aware of the unique qualities of the moment; open to possibilities; inquisitive; reverential; almost child-like in receptivity. The very opposite of a mind that is trapped and soured by the dullness of its own routine, that thinks it does not have to question things anymore, because it knows enough already.

The concepts of Esoterica, which represent a profound inheritance of Western culture, give us a glimpse into the deeper aspects of the quest. We have learned that truth, as *Aletheia*, is not just a reference to cold fact, but a subjective/objective encounter with reality that imbues our experience with the immediacy of life. The search for truth enriches us by pointing us away from personal stagnation.

The quest demands that we ask questions about truth. What is the subjective/objective experience of Aletheia? How does it change our conscious experience of the world?

*Question!*

*Areté* describes what is expected of us to reach our own human potential. Our morality must be based on the melding of virtue and reason. Until it does, we are dysfunctional and incomplete. We are called by nature to build upon our own potential in this regard, rationally developing our lives not only for ourselves but for the greater good.

The quest demands that we develop what is best about human nature. We must ask ourselves: how do we bring virtue to life through reason in our everyday lives?

*Question!*

*Telos* identifies the inner urge to grow and experience life fully, to utilize reason and virtue as a defining goal of personal fulfillment.

The quest demands that we listen to that inner voice as it encourages more consciousness and a mature relationship with our ideals. What do our deepest values and longings tell us to do?

*Question!*

We live in a state of constant change and motion that we refer to as time. *Kairos* tells us how each moment is uniquely important, and contributes to future change on the grandest scale. We are responsible for each decision that we make, and how it contributes to that future change. This is a charge that should not be taken lightly.

The quest demands that we look at the world as it develops around us. How do we contribute to that change to assure that the best of our ideals influence its direction?

And in the face of mystery, the mystery of our own existence, the quest demands that we ask the greatest questions of them all:

*What is the secret of the Grail? Whom does it serve?*

Visit www.chivalrynow.net to learn more about Chivalry-Now.

# Supplement 3: *Reference and Review*

### Chivalry-Now - Definition

Chivalry-Now is a code of ethics that embraces truth, self-discovery, reason and virtue that is deeply rooted in Western culture. It encourages us to find and enjoy personal authenticity by engaging everyday life as a quest.

It is also a worldwide fellowship of diverse people who are committed to healing our culture by returning what was lost – an updated mixture of Western realism and idealism for today's world.

Chivalry-Now calls for us to take back what was lost.

### The Quest

The hero's path. In mythology, the *quest* was a mission or journey of adventure in which the protagonist grows as a person and becomes more valuable to his or her community. We learn from this archetypal reference that when we approach life as a quest, as an on-going, learning experience, we live more consciously in the moment – we develop the skills and self-discipline necessary for a full and happy life that is dedicated to the greater good.

The quest teaches us purpose and meaning. When we fail to participate in the quest, our lives become smaller, repetitive, and influenced by a conflict of values that impedes spiritual growth and personal fulfillment.

### Esoterica

Esoterica reclaims the *Philosophical Treasures* of Western culture bequeathed to us by our history. They explore the depth and form the basis of Chivalry-Now as the heir and vehicle of those treasures, and serve as its legitimate pedigree. For those who aspire to be companions or knights of this fellowship, a solid understanding of these principles is vital. To the open mind they are morally and spiritually transforming.

To assist the reader in remembering the tenets of Esoterica, we offer this quick reference and review:

## Aletheia
A concept that brings together the subjective and objective experiences of Truth that makes the quest a fulfilling growth experience.

## Areté
The *greatest good* or *highest virtue*. The excellent functioning of the most recognized trait of a species. For human beings, this is a combination of reason and virtue.

## Anagnorisis
A sudden clarity of vision that pierces the falsehood of illusion and produces a sudden awakening of consciousness as a kind of rebirth.

## Telos
The inner aim of a living creature that produces its own natural development.

## Responsibility
Existentialism describes responsibility as more than a moment's culpability; it is a way of life that makes true freedom possible.

## Ordo Mundi

The Way of the World. Nature, and our relationship to nature. Theologically, Ordo Mundi was considered a direct revelation from God

## Nature's Law

A marriage of reason and virtue that guides and fulfills human nature. (Areté is the excellent functioning of Nature's Law in human beings.)

## Reason

The application of sensible logic to human thought.

## Grail Consciousness

Living fully in the moment while relating to mystery at the same time.

## Kairos

A significant, sometimes almost global, event in which many disparate factors combine to produce an evolutionary leap in human consciousness.

# B O O K S